monday morning®

D1297874

Center Connections

by Shirley Ross and Mary Ann Hawke
illustrated by Marilynn Barr

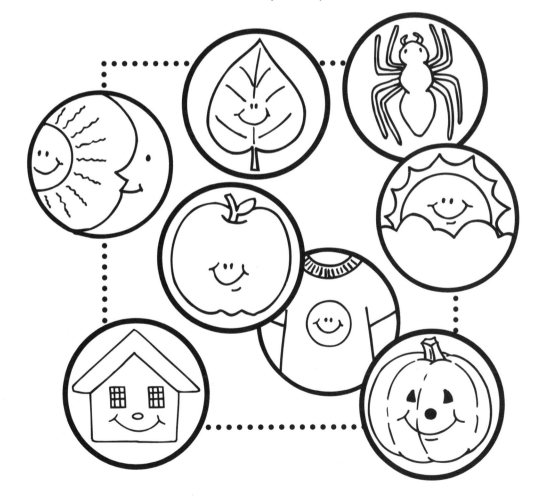

Publisher: Roberta Suid
Copy Editor: Carol Whiteley
Production: MGB Press
Cover Design: David Hale

For a complete catalog, please write to the address below:
P.O. Box 1680
Palo Alto, CA 94302

Call our toll-free number: 1-800-255-6049
E-mail us at: MMBooks@aol.com
Visit our Web site:
http://www.mondaymorningbooks.com

Monday Morning Books is a registered trademark of
Monday Morning Books, Inc.

ISBN 1-57612-049-X
Printed in the United States of America

9876543

CONTENTS

INTRODUCTION

From the Authors

"Center time" is one of our students' favorite times in the school day (just a step below "free choice" time). Because of this interest we have gathered together lots of centers-related ideas through the years, resulting in this book, *Center Connections*.

We have enjoyed putting these materials together. We hope that you and your students have as much pleasure using them as we have had creating them.

To the Teacher

Center Connections is divided into four sections based on the seasons of the year. Included in each section is a page of activities to help the students understand and enjoy that season, such as a "signs of autumn" walk, a mural depicting the activities of the season to make together and post in the classroom, a related poem poster for the children to illustrate, and special monthly playhouse transformations to create the seasonal atmosphere in the classroom.

There are 14 weekly mini study units in the book—four per season except for summer, which has two. Each unit has a circle time activity designed to introduce the theme during group time, a book list for the classroom reading corner and to use for group story time, and center activities for science, literature, art, math, and reading.

The Centers

Each center description includes a list of materials to be gathered for the activity, notes about teacher preparation, and a blackline master for a student poster that gives simple directions for the activity. Make a copy of the poster on tagboard. Read it with the students as you demonstrate the activity for them, then post it in the center.

As center materials are gathered, place them in labelled plastic dishpans or litter boxes, one for each center. Since classroom space is often limited, this allows the centers to be portable and to be located on a desk top, area rug, or table.

The Reading Center is a little different than the other centers. Here the children color and add special touches to their own eight-page mini reader, the text of which has been introduced to them prior to the theme's centers and has been read to them many times from a class big book. The children will make finger puppets called Pointer Pals to use as they read their completed books.

Class Big Books

Introduce the big book to the children one or two weeks before you begin the related theme centers. Then you can read it to them many times before they make their own books to read for themselves.

Start by reading the book to the whole class, pointing to each of the words with your Pointer Pal (see the Pointer Pal section for directions on how to make them). Do this at group listening times. At another sitting, read one line at a time and have the children echo your reading as you point. The next step is for you and your children to read together as you point, with the children filling in a word or phrase that you point to but don't say. Finally, have the children read together as you point only.

To make each class big book, copy the blacklines onto white construction paper (12" x 9") and color the pictures using your own choice of media. For durability laminate the pages before binding them down the left side.

Student Readers

These books are for early learners—four-, five-, and some six-year-olds. It is best that the teacher or an adult volunteer assemble them. The children will be coloring them and adding special touches, but they are really too young to cut the pages evenly or to put them in numerical order. During the appropriate theme week, put the assembled books in the Book-Making Center for the children to color and add special touches to.

Make enough copies of the blackline masters so that each child will have an eight-page book, and so that there are at least two extras for the class library.

Special Note to the Book Assembler

To cut the pages apart so that they are all the same size, cut the duplicated copies exactly in half both the long way of the paper and the short. Use a paper cutter with rulers along the side to measure the pages. Each page should be cut in half, first horizontally and then vertically.

Plan for the children to go to the Book-Making Center daily. During group time, read the class big book together, show the children which two pages they will color at the center, and how to put the "special touch" in place when the appropriate day arrives. We find that it is best to limit the number of pages colored per day to no more than one or two. This helps to eliminate hurried scribbling and adds to the number of days that the children have to practice reading their books at school. Have each child read his or her book after doing the daily center assignment and before leaving the center.

When all the books are completed, send them home. Encourage the children to read their books for at least another week to someone who will listen each day.

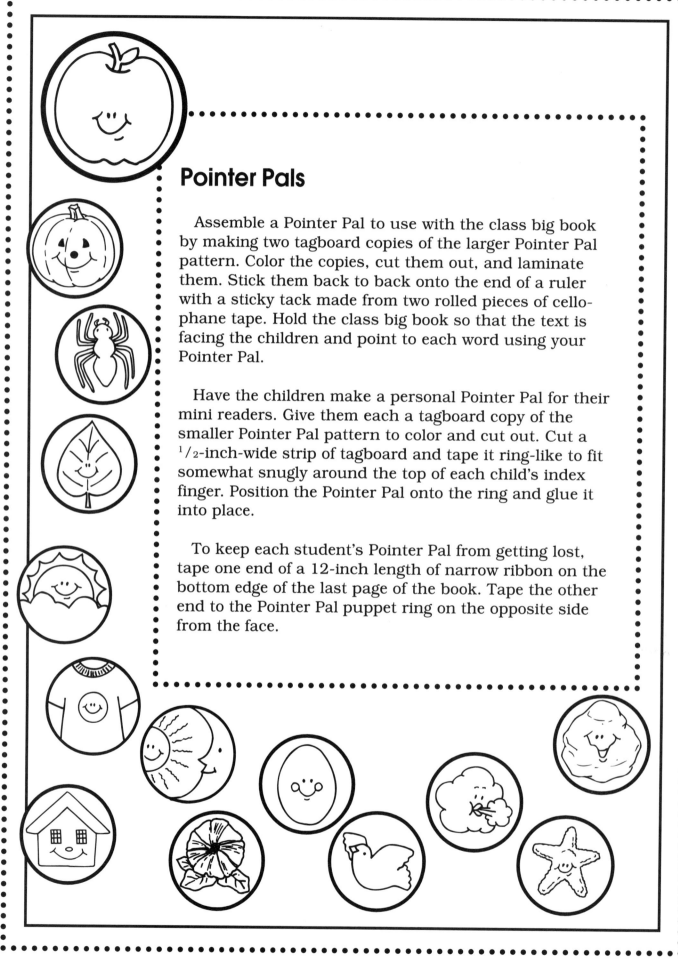

Pointer Pals

Assemble a Pointer Pal to use with the class big book by making two tagboard copies of the larger Pointer Pal pattern. Color the copies, cut them out, and laminate them. Stick them back to back onto the end of a ruler with a sticky tack made from two rolled pieces of cellophane tape. Hold the class big book so that the text is facing the children and point to each word using your Pointer Pal.

Have the children make a personal Pointer Pal for their mini readers. Give them each a tagboard copy of the smaller Pointer Pal pattern to color and cut out. Cut a $1/2$-inch-wide strip of tagboard and tape it ring-like to fit somewhat snugly around the top of each child's index finger. Position the Pointer Pal onto the ring and glue it into place.

To keep each student's Pointer Pal from getting lost, tape one end of a 12-inch length of narrow ribbon on the bottom edge of the last page of the book. Tape the other end to the Pointer Pal puppet ring on the opposite side from the face.

AUTUMN

Read a book about the seasons to the children. Take a walk together to look for signs of autumn.

Mural

Paint grass and bare trees on a large piece of butcher paper. Have each of the children make a picture of him- or herself playing or raking leaves to cut out and glue onto the background. Put out autumn-colored construction paper and let the children tear it into small leaf-shaped pieces to glue on the trees and the grass.

Poetry Poster

Copy the nursery rhyme "Peter, Peter, Pumpkin Eater" onto heavy paper. Post it at the children's eye level and decorate it with paper pumpkins the children have made. Have them make cut-out pictures of Peter's wife to stick out of the pumpkin tops.

Playhouse Transformations

September is the time of the year when the housekeeping corner should be just a playhouse with a small table and chairs, stove, sink, refrigerator, dolls, doll beds, a telephone, and utensils.

October is Halloween month. Have children make paper bag jack-o'-lanterns and black and orange paper chains for decorations. Have them make black spiders and hang some of them in the October housekeeping corner. Put some old sheets (ghost costumes) in the dress-up box.

In early November read a book to the children about Pilgrim life. Make "candles" for the November housekeeping corner from toilet tissue tubes with a piece of orange tissue paper sticking out of the top. Remove the modern furniture and replace it with a fireplace made from a cardboard box and "fire" created from rolled brown construction paper logs with crumpled orange tissue paper on top. It would be fun for the children to make paper Pilgrim hats and collars to wear in their log cabin replica.

APPLES

Circle Time

Bring three or four different kinds of apples to the classroom for the children to see and taste (examples: Red Delicious, Granny Smith, Macintosh, Golden Delicious). Discuss how the apples are alike and how they are different. Have apples from each variety precut into small pieces for the children to taste. Encourage the children to try each kind, so they can decide which they like best. Graph the children's answers to the question "Which apple did I like best?" *The Seasons of Arnold's Apple Tree* by Gail Gibbons is a great book to read after the apple tasting. It tells about a little boy's special bond with an apple tree throughout the changing seasons.

Teach the children the following finger play:

Way up in the apple tree (point up in the air)
Five little apples smiled at me (hold up 5 fingers).
I shook that tree just as hard as I could (pretend to shake a tree),
Down came one apple—umm, it was good!
(Pretend to pick up an apple and eat it.)
(Repeat the verse four more times with 4, 3, 2, and 1 apples.)

Explain the center activities.

 ## Book List

Apple Picking Time by Michele Benoit (Crown, 1994).
Apple Tree by Barrie Watts (Silver Burdett, 1986).
Apple Valley Year by Ann Turner (Macmillan, 1993).
Johnny Appleseed by Steven Kellogg (Morrow, 1988).
The Seasons of Arnold's Apple Tree by Gail Gibbons (Harcourt Brace Jovanovich, 1984).
The Story of Johnny Appleseed by Aliki (Prentice-Hall, 1933).

Johnny Appleseed

Materials

Listening post and earphones
Cassette recorder and blank cassette tape
At least one copy of the book *The Story of Johnny Appleseed* by Aliki or *Johnny Appleseed* by Steven Kellogg
Drawing paper and crayons

Teacher's Notes

• Record the story.
• Explain to the children that they will be listening to a story about a man who lived long ago. Tell them that his real name was John Chapman, but that people called him Johnny Appleseed. Ask them to listen carefully to the story to find out how he got his nickname.
• After listening to the story, have children make a picture of Johnny Appleseed that tells how he got his name.

Johnny Appleseed

1. Listen quietly to the story.

2. Talk about the story with the listener sitting next to you. Find out how Johnny Appleseed got his nickname.

3. Make a picture of Johnny Appleseed. Draw something in your picture that tells about his nickname.

4. Put your name on your picture.

Fingerprint Apple Trees

Materials

Construction paper (9" x 12", white or
   light blue)
Dark green paper (tissue, art, or
   construction paper)
Brown felt markers
Glue
Red tempera paint

Teacher's Notes

• Gather the suggested materials together. Prepare and display
   the center poster.
• Demonstrate the center activity for the children. Make an example
   of the project to place in the center.

Fingerprint Apple Trees

1. Use a brown marker to draw the tree trunk and branches.

2. Make leaves by tearing the green paper into small pieces.

3. Glue the leaves onto the tree branches.

4. Dip your finger into red paint and print apples on the tree.

5. Sign your work of art. (Write your name on your paper.)

Apples, Apples, More Apples

Materials

Apples, Apples, More Apples playing cards

Teacher's Notes

• Gather the materials and prepare the center poster for display.
• Make two copies of the playing card activity page on oak tag for each child.
• Review the concept of "more and less."
• Show children how to play the game. Make a sample set of cards to display in the center.

Apples, Apples, More Apples

1. Color the apple playing cards. Cut apart.

2. Find a partner to play the apple card game with. Use only one player's cards.

To start the game:
- Shuffle the cards.
- Deal out all the cards.
- The players put their cards in a pile face down in front of them.

To play the game:
- Each player turns over the top card in his/her pile.
- The player whose card has more apples on it takes both cards and puts them face up in front of her/him.
- Do these two steps until both players' face-down cards have been turned over.
- The player with the most cards wins.

Apple Playing Cards

Apples, Apples, More Apples	O ... O	1 ... 1	2 ... 2
3 ... 3	4 ... 4	5 ... 5	6 ... 6
7 ... 7	8 ... 8	9 ... 9	10 ... 10

Seasons of an Apple Tree

Materials

Bare tree trunk and branches pattern
Light blue construction paper
Brown crayons
Tempera paint—pink, green, red, orange,
   and yellow
Small pieces of sponge about 1" square,
   1 per color of paint
Stapler and staples

Teacher's Notes

• Make four copies of the bare tree pattern on light blue
   construction paper.
• Gather the materials and prepare the center poster for display.
• Talk about the seasons of the year and how the apple tree changes
   during them. Show the children pictures from a seasonal book
   such as *The Seasons of Arnold's Apple Tree* by Gail Gibbons.
• Make a model of the center project with the children, discussing
   each of the steps. Leave it on display in the center.

Seasons of an Apple Tree

1. Color the trunk and branches of all four trees brown.
2. Sponge-paint pink blossoms on one of the tree branches for spring.
3. Sponge-paint green leaves on another tree for summer.
4. When the green paint dries, make red finger-print apples among the leaves for summer.
5. Sponge-paint yellow, orange, and red leaves on another tree for autumn.
6. When the paint dries, arrange the trees in order by season and ask a helper to staple them into a book.

    First page—Spring
    Second page—Summer
    Third page—Autumn
    Fourth page—Winter

7. Write the name of the season on each page.
8. Make a cover for your book. Write your name in the title:

The Seasons of _____'s Apple Tree

Tree Pattern

Apples! Apples!

Materials

Assembled student readers
Crayons
Ground cinnamon
White glue
Tagboard copies of the little Pointer Pal
    pattern, 1 per student
Strips of tagboard
Cellophane tape
Narrow-tip colored felt pens (for Pointer Pals)
Lengths of narrow ribbon, 1 per student
Scissors

• •

Teacher's Notes for Student Readers

• Make copies of the student readers and assemble one per child.
  See directions for assembling in the Introduction.
• Show the children which pages to color—two each day.

• •

Special Touch: When the children have finished coloring their
readers, let them glue a small sprinkling of cinnamon on the picture
of the pie on page 5. Be sure they leave their books open until the
glue dries.

• •

Notes for Pointer Pals

• After the children have completed their readers, put the materials
  for making the Pointer Pals in the Reading Center and show the
  children how to color and cut them out.
• Have an adult volunteer complete the students' Pointer Pals as
  described in the Introduction.

Pointer Pal Patterns ⫸

Apples! Apples

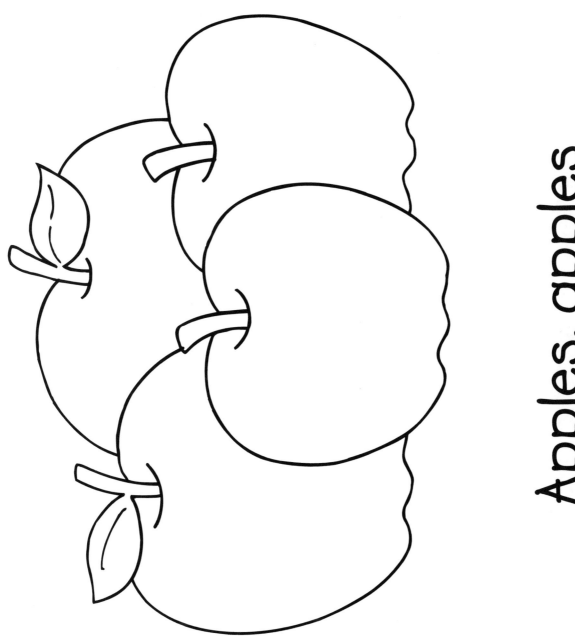

Apples, apples

1.

Here is a red apple.

2.

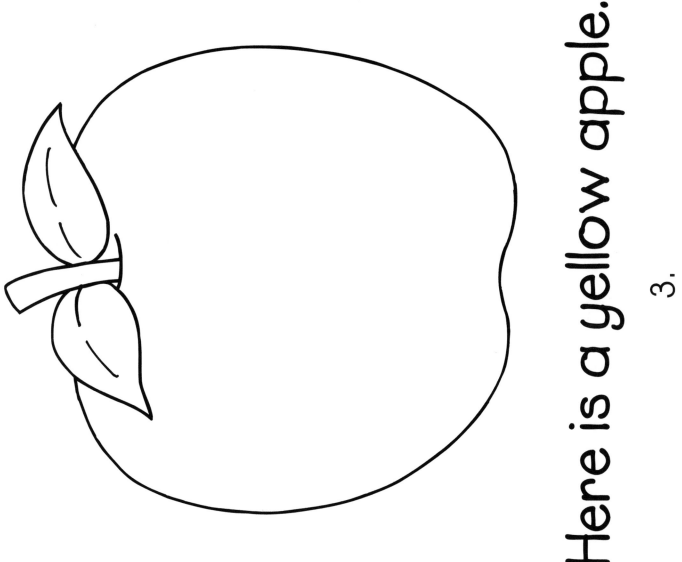

Here is a yellow apple.

3.

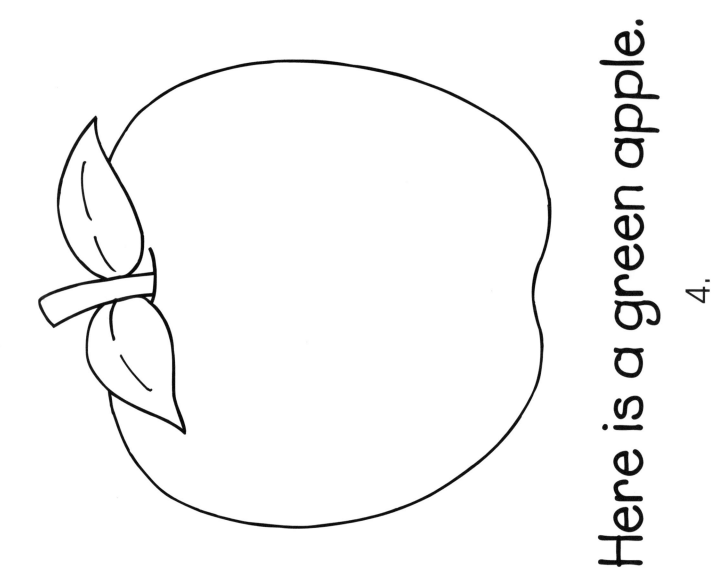

Here is a green apple.

4.

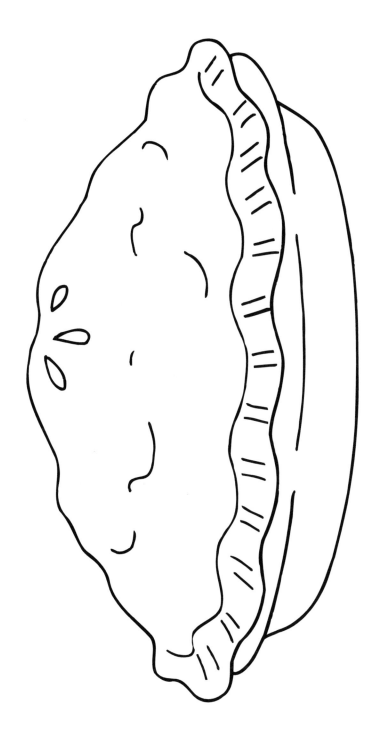

Here is an apple pie.

5.

 Center Connections ©1998 Monday Morning Books, Inc.

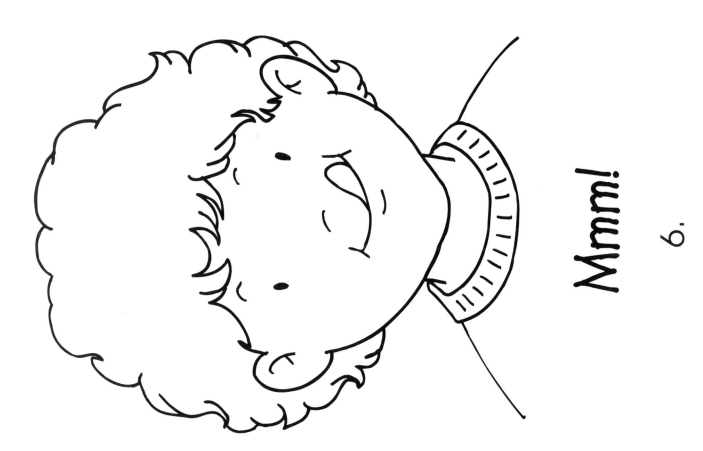

Mmm!

6.

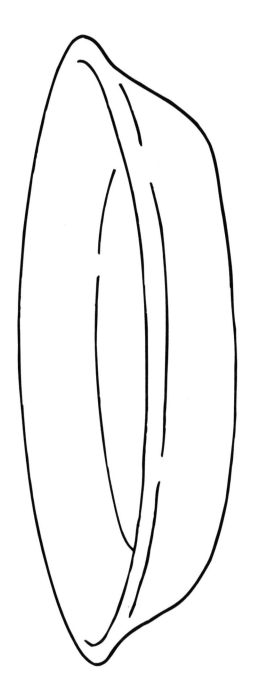

No more apples.

7.

Apples! Apples

Apples, apples

1.

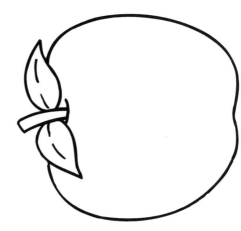

Here is a yellow apple.

3.

Here is a red apple.

2.

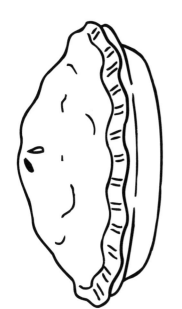

Here is a green apple.

4.

Here is an apple pie.

5.

Mmm!

6.

No more apples.

7.

PUMPKINS

Circle Time

Introduce the pumpkin centers by bringing to the classroom several real pumpkins. Try to find a variety of sizes and shapes including, if possible, one that is still green. Put the pumpkins in a large box and, as you dramatically pull each pumpkin out of the box, say the following rhyme:

Pumpkin large (take out a large pumpkin),
Pumpkin small (take out a small pumpkin),
Pumpkin short (continue to take out the pumpkins to match
   the verse or point to the one that has the characteristic),
Pumpkin tall,
Pumpkin orange,
Pumpkin green.
These are the pumpkins I have seen.

Discuss how the pumpkins are different and how they are the same.

Explain the procedures and activities in the four pumpkin centers.

 ## Book List

The Biggest Pumpkin Ever by Steven Kroll (Scholastic, 1984).
It's a Fruit, It's a Vegetable, It's a Pumpkin by Allan Fowler
   (Children's Press, 1995).
It's Pumpkin Time by Zoe Hall (Scholastic, 1994).
Mousekin's Golden House by Edna Miller (Simon and
   Schuster, 1984).
The Pumpkin Man from Piney Creek by Darleen Baily Beard
   (Simon and Schuster, 1995).
Pumpkin Patch by Elizabeth King (Dutton, 1990).
Pumpkin, Pumpkin by Jeanne Titherington (Greenwillow,
   1986).

Pumpkin, Pumpkin

Materials

Listening post and earphones
Tape recorder and blank cassette tape
At least one copy of the book *Pumpkin,*
  Pumpkin by Jeanne Titherington
Drawing paper and crayons

Teacher's Notes

- Make a tape recording of the story.
- Gather the materials. Prepare and display the center poster.
- Tell the children that the pictures in *Pumpkin, Pumpkin* tell the story as well as the words. Encourage the children to look at the pictures in the book carefully after they listen to the story.
- Review the listening directions on the poster.

Pumpkin, Pumpkin

1. Listen quietly to the story. Look at the pictures too.

2. Talk to a listener sitting next to you about what Jamie did to help his pumpkin grow.

3. Pretend you are Jamie. Draw a picture of yourself with the pumpkin you grew.

4. Write your name on your picture.

Our Pumpkin Patch

Materials

Various sizes of grocery-style paper bags
Lots of newspaper
Green yarn
Orange tempera paint and brushes
Green construction paper
Glue
Scissors

Teacher's Notes

- Cut the yarn into 36-inch lengths for the pumpkin vines.
- Gather the materials. Prepare and display the center poster.
- Show the children that the pictures in *Pumpkin, Pumpkin* tell the story as well as the words.
- Show how to wad up a sheet of newspaper into a ball to stuff into their bags. Tell them it will take many newspaper balls to make the "pumpkin" nice and plump.
- Help the children twist the tops of their bags shut and tie the green string (vine) around them. (This would be a good activity to invite a parent volunteer to participate in.)
- Show the children some real pumpkin leaves if possible and point out their shape. Make green construction paper copies of the pumpkin leaf activity page if no real leaves are available. Make an example of the stuffed pumpkin to put in the center.
- When the pumpkins are complete, transform the classroom into a pumpkin patch by placing the children's creations on window sills, counters, and out-of-the-way corners of the room. Include vines and leaves too.

Our Pumpkin Patch

1. Choose a bag to make into a pumpkin. Stuff it with newspaper balls.

2. Twist the top of the bag when it is full. Tie a piece of green yarn around it.

3. Paint your "pumpkin" orange.

4. Cut out some green leaves and glue them onto your pumpkin's vine.

Pumpkin Leaf

Pumpkin Weigh-in

Materials

Small pumpkins (1 per child at the center)
Balance scale (1 per child at the center)
A copy of the activity page for each child
Pencils
Sets of objects to balance against the
   pumpkin (wooden blocks, uniflex cubes,
   teddy bear counters, scissors, etc.)

Teacher's Notes

- Gather the materials. Prepare and display the center poster.
- Teach the children how the balance scale works. Show them how
  to put the pumpkin in the tray on one side and put one object at
  a time on the other side until the pumpkin is straight across from
  the other objects.
- Demonstrate the activity step by step.

Pumpkin Weigh-in

1. Put a pumpkin on one side of the balance scale.

2. Put one block at a time into the tray on the other side of the balance scale until both trays are straight across from each other.

3. Count the blocks on the tray and write the number on your recording page. Draw a picture of a block next to the number.

4. Take the first set of things off the scale and balance another set of objects with the pumpkin. Count how many it takes to balance with the pumpkin and write the number. Draw a picture of one of the objects from that set next to the number.

5. Do the same thing two more times using a different set of objects each time.

Name _____

Pumpkin Weigh-in

_____

_____

_____

_____

Pumpkin Headbands

Materials

Brown and white construction paper
Rubber bands
Pumpkin seeds
Green yarn
Scissors
Glue
Stapler and staples

Teacher's Notes

• Prepare the materials:
  — Cut the brown construction paper into strips 3" x 18" (one per child).
  — Make copies of the pumpkin life cycle patterns on white construction paper (one per child).
  — Cut the green yarn into 16" lengths (one per child).
• Prepare and display the center poster.
• Use the life cycle drawings to make a life cycle chart and discuss the growth sequence of a pumpkin seed to a pumpkin.
• Demonstrate the steps of the center activity. Make a model of the headband to display in the center.
• As the children finish their headbands, staple a rubber band to one end of the brown strip. Then bring the other end of the strip around to form a circle and staple the other end of the rubber band to that end of the paper strip (a simple way to make sure the headband fits).

← Staple.

Staple.

Pumpkin Headbands

1. Lay the brown paper strip on the table in front of you.
2. Start on the left and glue a pumpkin seed on the strip.
3. Cut out the seedling with two leaves and glue it next to the seed.
4. Make a curvy line with the glue along the rest of the brown strip. Lay the green yarn on top of the glue line. This will be the pumpkin vine.
5. Cut out some green leaves and glue them along the vine.
6. Color the star-shaped flower yellow. Cut it out and glue it on the vine nearest the sprouts.
7. Color the "baby" pumpkin green. Cut it out and glue it to the vine next to the yellow flower.
8. Color the big pumpkin orange. Cut it out and glue it next to the baby pumpkin on the vine.
9. A grown-up will fasten your headband together for you to wear.

Pumpkin Life Cycle Patterns

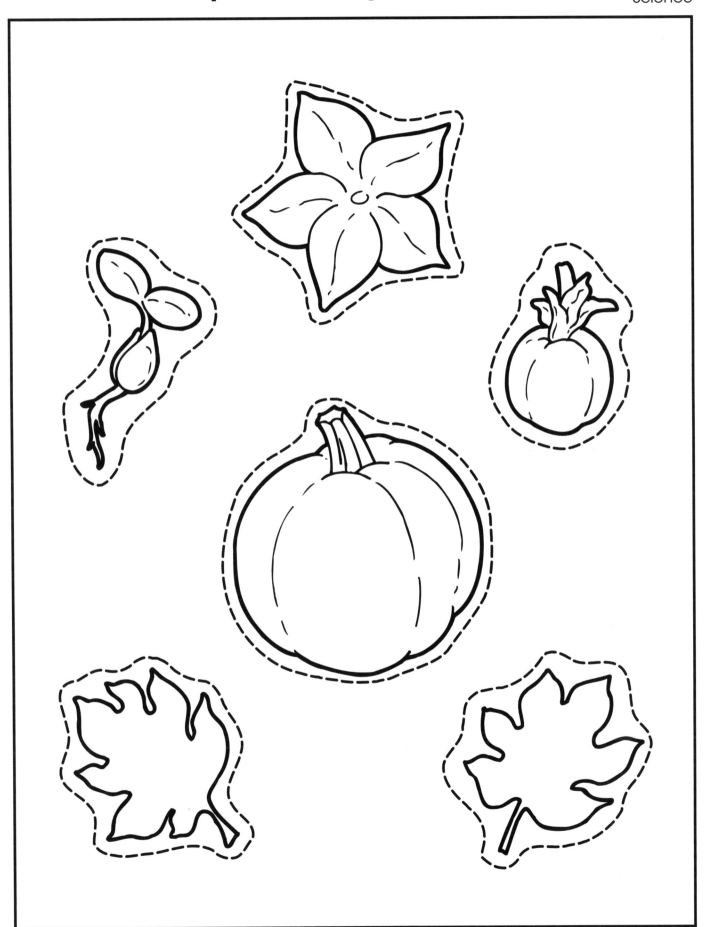

Pumpkins for Sale

Materials

Assembled student readers
Crayons
Pumpkin pie spice
White glue
Tagboard copies of the little Pointer Pal
   pattern, 1 per student
Strips of tagboard
Cellophane tape
Narrow-tip colored felt pens (for Pointer Pals)
Lengths of narrow ribbon, 1 per student
Scissors

Teacher's Notes for Student Readers

- Gather the materials.
- Make copies of the student readers and assemble one per child.
  See directions for assembling in the Introduction.
- Show the children which two pages to color each day.

Special Touch: When the children have finished coloring their
readers, have them spread a small amount of glue on the picture of
the pumpkin pie slice on page 7 and sprinkle a tiny bit of pumpkin
pie spice on it. Be sure the glue is dry before closing the book.

Notes for Pointer Pals

- When the student readers are complete, put the materials for
  making the Pointer Pals in the Reading Center and show the
  children how to color and cut them out.
- Have an adult volunteer complete the students' Pointer Pals as
  described in the Introduction.

Pointer Pal Patterns ➥

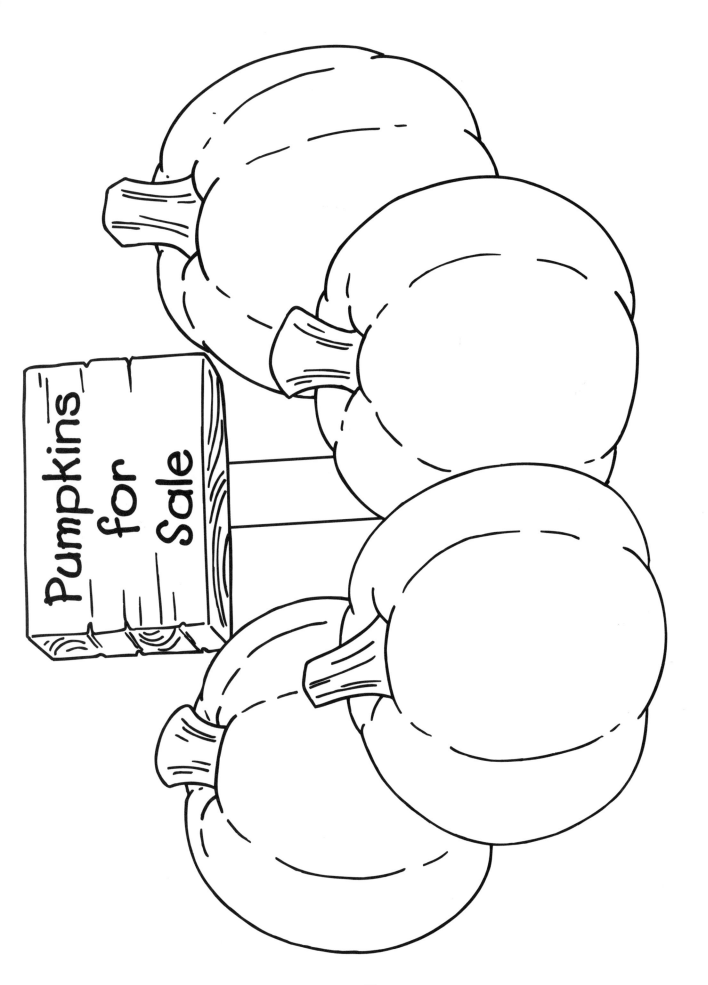

Pumpkins for Sale

Center Connections ©1998 Monday Morning Books, Inc.

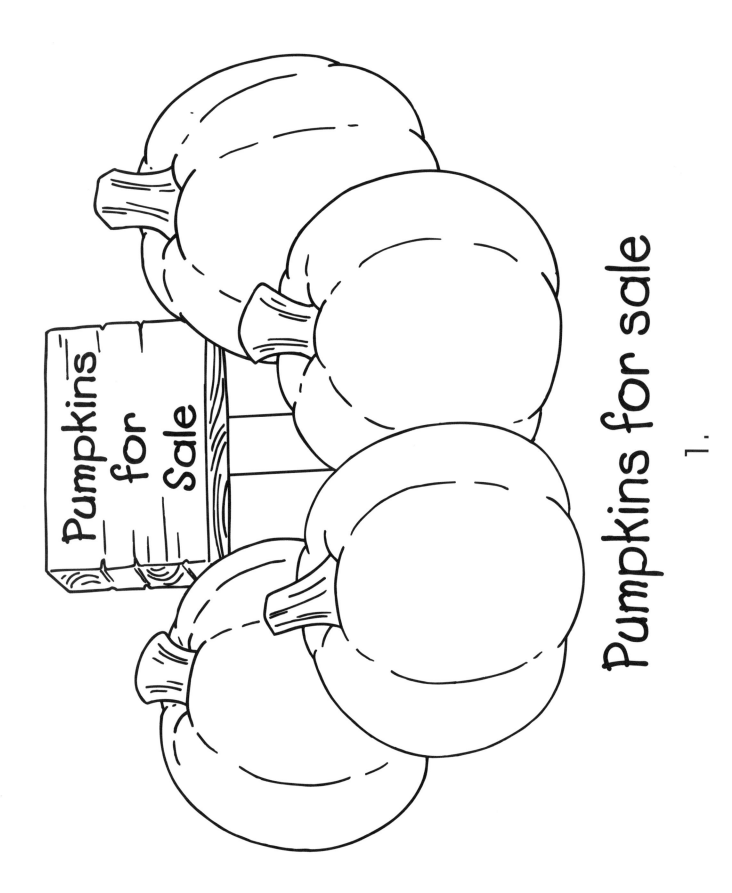

Pumpkins for Sale

Pumpkins for sale

1.

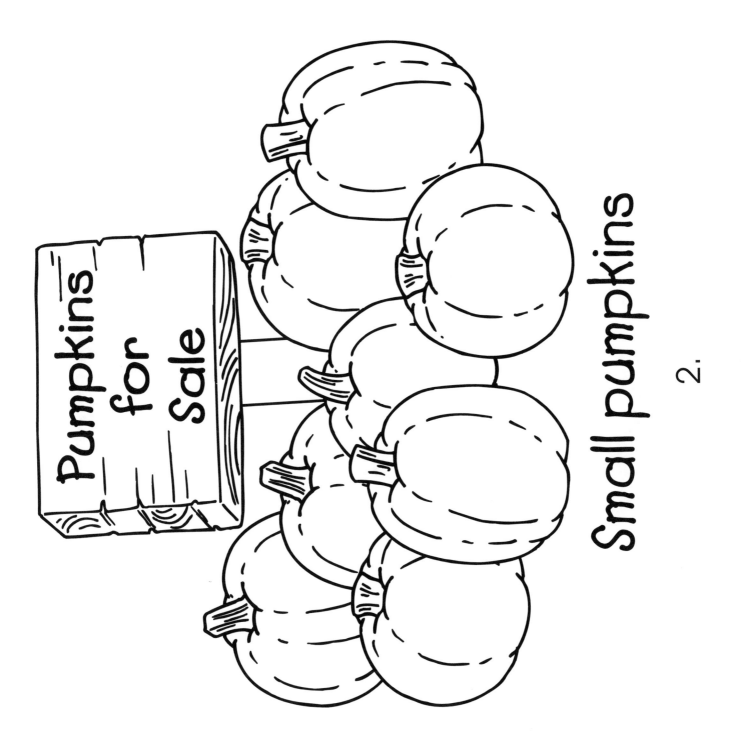

Small pumpkins

2.

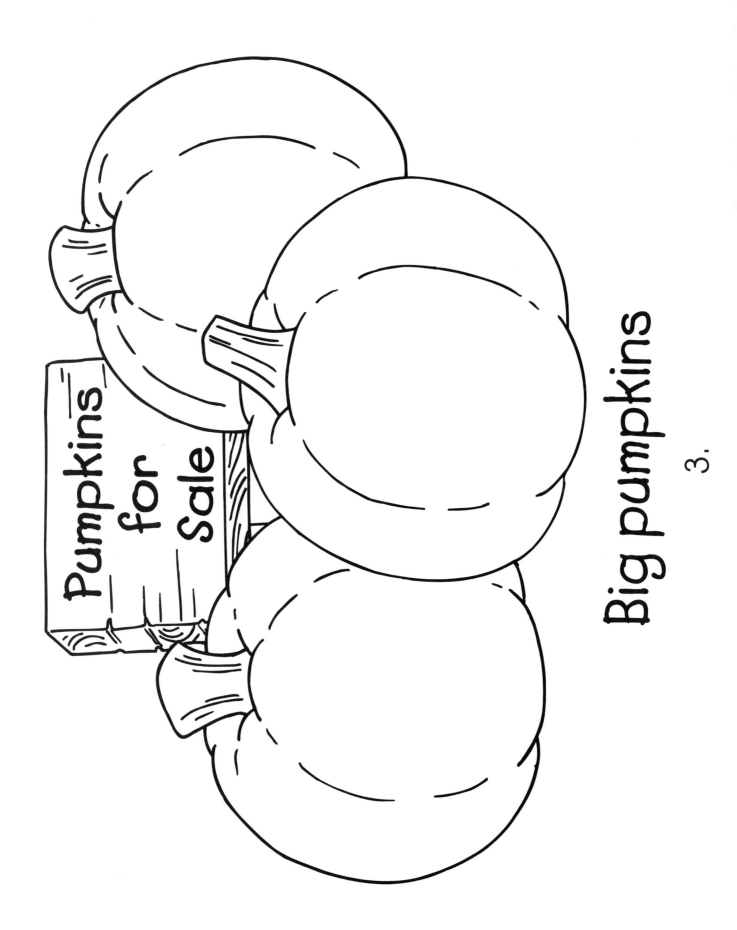

Pumpkins for Sale

3. Big pumpkins

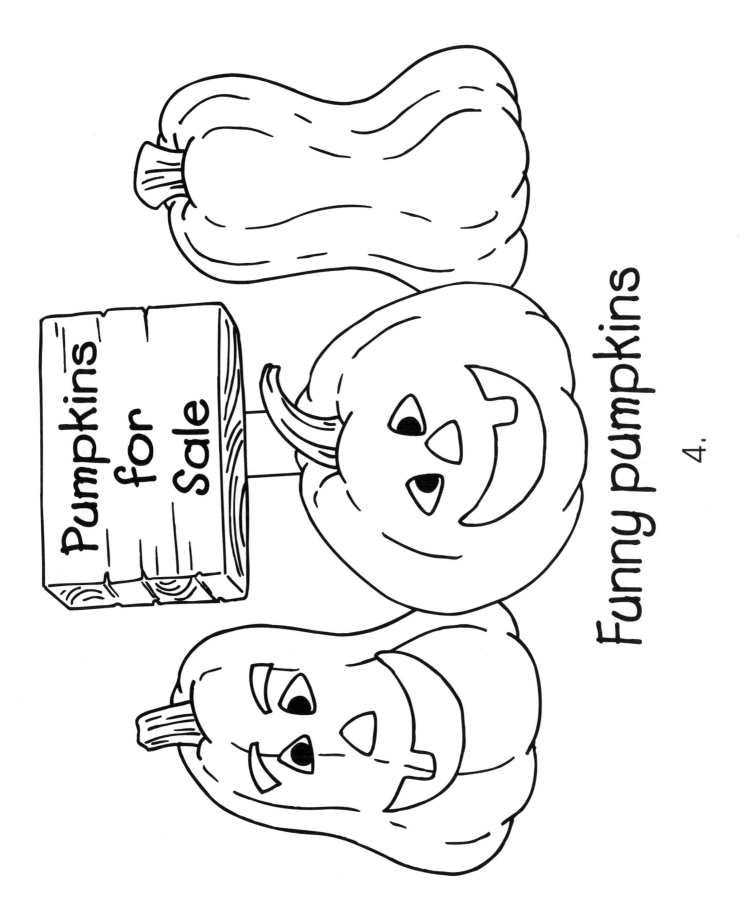

Funny pumpkins

4.

Scary pumpkins

5.

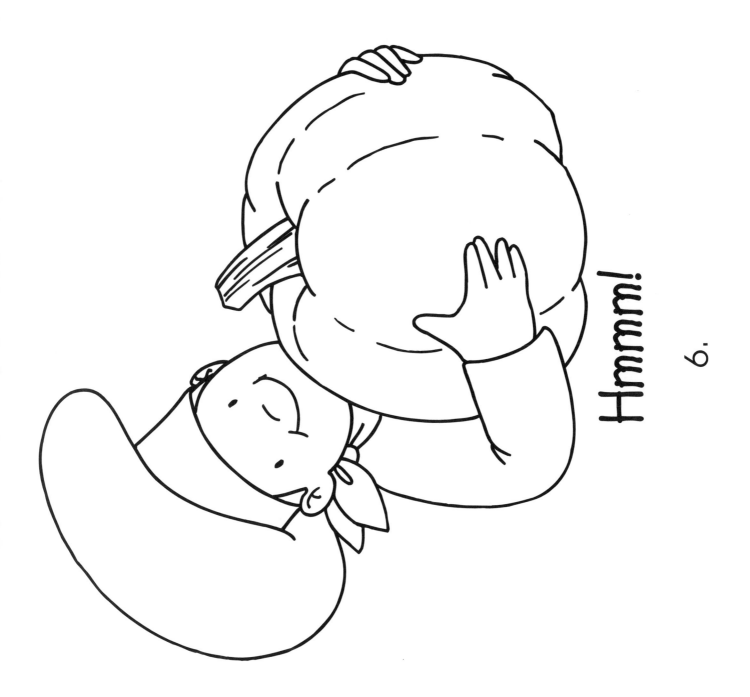

Hmmm!

6.

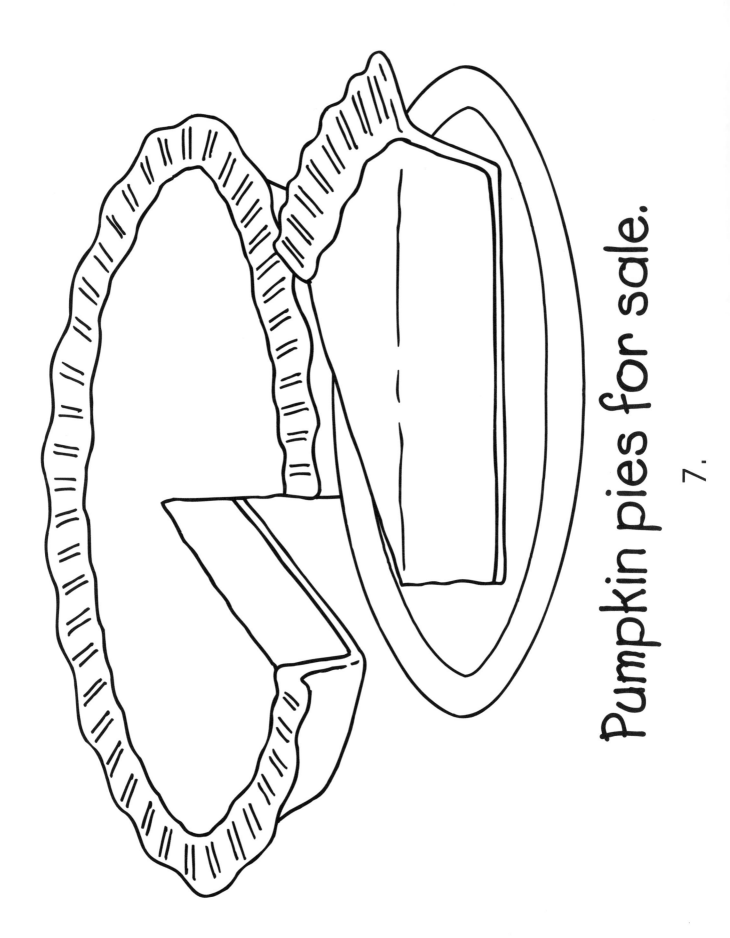

Pumpkin pies for sale.

7.

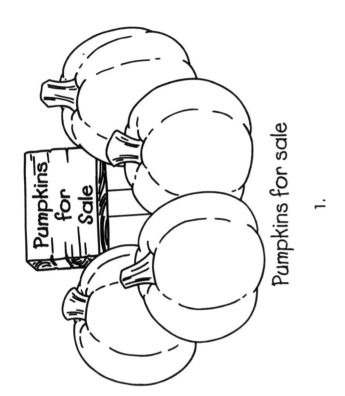

Pumpkins for sale

1.

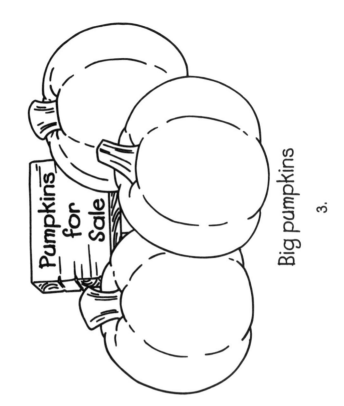

Big pumpkins

3.

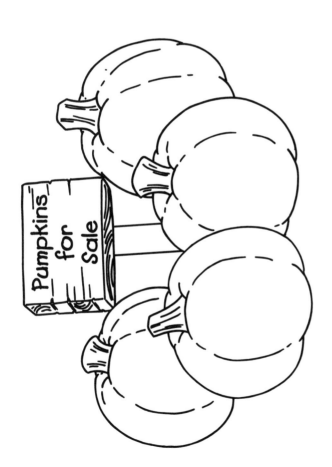

Small pumpkins

2.

Scary pumpkins

5.

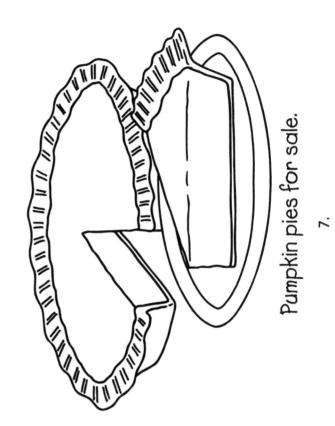

Pumpkin pies for sale.

7.

Funny pumpkins

4.

Hmmm!

6.

 # SPIDERS

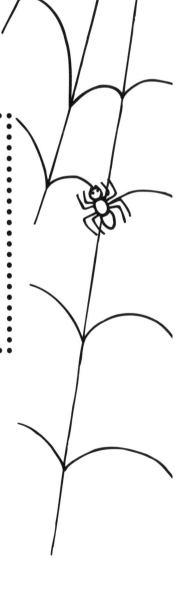

Circle Time

Children often have mixed feeling about spiders. They are fascinated by the little creatures, but are also fearful of them. Begin the study of spiders by acknowledging that fear with a class graph entitled "Are You Afraid of Spiders?" Keep the graph to refer to later. Some children will have changed their minds by the end of the study. Be sure to caution children that some spiders are poisonous, and if touched may bite. Inform them about any poisonous spiders in your area. Discuss precautions that should be taken, such as, "Don't reach into dark corners in garages, basements, or wood piles." Consult your local librarian for reference books about spiders, or note the following book list. Show children pictures of spiders and point out their beneficial role in nature.

Explain the center activities, modeling the procedures when necessary.

 ## Book List

Ananzi, the Spider by Gerald McDermott (Henry Holt, 1972).
Be Nice to Spiders by Margaret Graham (Harper Collins, 1967).
Itsy Bitsy Spider by Iza Trapani (Whispering Coyote Press, 1993).
Spider's Web by Barrie Watts and Christine Back (Silver Burdett, 1984).
The Very Busy Spider by Eric Carle (Philomel, 1984).

The Very Busy Spider

Materials

Listening post and earphones
Tape recorder and blank cassette tape
At least one copy of the book
The Very Busy Spider by Eric Carle
Black construction paper
Rubber bands
Glue
Stapler and staples
Scissors

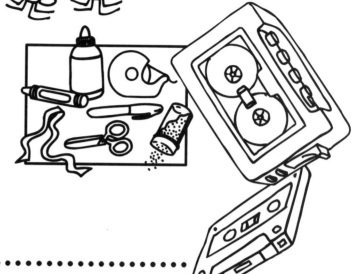

Teacher's Notes

• Make a tape recording of the story.
• Cut the black construction paper into strips 2" x 18" (1 per child) and 1" x 9" (8 per child).
• Make a spider headband to display in the center.
• When the children have finished gluing the eight legs (the shorter strips) around the longer headband strip, finish the headbands by bringing the two ends of the longer strip around to form a circle. Staple one end of a rubber band to one end of the paper strip and the other end of the rubber band to the other end of the strip.

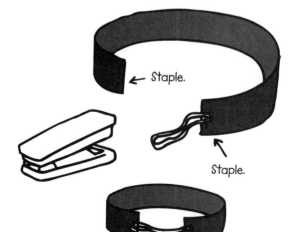

Staple.

Staple.

56

The Very Busy Spider

1. Listen quietly to the story. Look at the pictures in the book.

2. Tell a friend how many legs you saw on the very busy spider.

3. Make a spider headband:
   - Take one long strip of black paper.
   - Count out eight short strips and fold them in half.
   - Glue the short-strip legs along the long headband strip.
   - Ask a grown-up to finish the headband for you.

Spider Webs

Materials

Foil pie pans, 1 per child
Black construction paper circles, 1 per child
Marbles
White liquid tempera paint
Salt
Scissors
Shallow paint containers

Teacher's Notes

- Gather the materials. Prepare and display the center poster.
- Cut circles from black construction paper the same size as the bottoms of the pie pans.
- Prepare the paint by mixing the tempera with a little table salt. The salt will crystallize as it dries, adding some sparkle to the web.
- Put the paint mixture into a shallow container so that a marble can be retrieved easily after it has been thoroughly coated with paint. Show the children how to roll a marble around in the paint to coat it, then fish it out and drop it onto the black circle that has been placed in the bottom of the pie pan.
- Model the process from start to finish. Make a sample of the project to display in the center.

Spider Webs

1. Put a black paper circle in the bottom of a pie pan.

2. Drop a marble into white paint. Roll it around so that it is covered with paint.

3. Use your fingers to lift the marble out of the paint and drop it onto the black paper in the pie pan.

4. Make the marble roll around by carefully tipping the pie pan back and forth.

5. Let your spider web design dry.

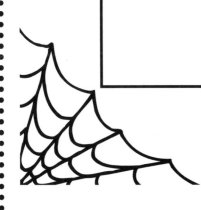

Spider Stories

Materials

Spider web story mat
Plastic spiders (usually available at variety, hobby, or craft stores)
Spider cards
Tagboard
Scissors
Crayons (optional)

Once there was one spider on a web. Two more spiders came to join her.

Teacher's Notes

- Make one copy per child of the spider web story mat on tagboard.
- If plastic spiders are not available, duplicate 5 to 10 spider cards onto tagboard for the children to color and cut apart for their spider stories.
- Model the center activity by telling several math stories using the story mat and spiders to act them out.
- Prepare and display the center poster.

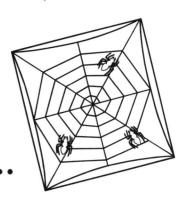

Examples of Spider Number Stories

- Once there was one spider on a web. (Put one on the web story mat.) Two more spiders came out to join her. (Put two more spiders on the mat.) Ask, "How many are on the web now?"
- Five spiders were playing on their web one day. (Put five spiders on the web.) One of the spiders decided to go visit a friend. (Take one spider away.) Ask, "How many are left on the web?"

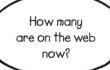

How many are on the web now?

Five spiders were playing on their web one day. One of the spiders decided to go visit a friend.

How many are left on the web?

60

Spider Stories

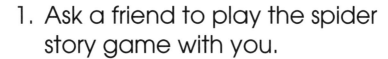

1. Ask a friend to play the spider story game with you.

2. Think of a number story about 1, 2, 3, 4, or 5 spiders to tell a friend. As you tell it let your friend act it out with the spiders on the spider web story mat.

3. Take turns telling more spider stories with the spider web story mat and the spiders.

Spider Web Story Mat
and Cards

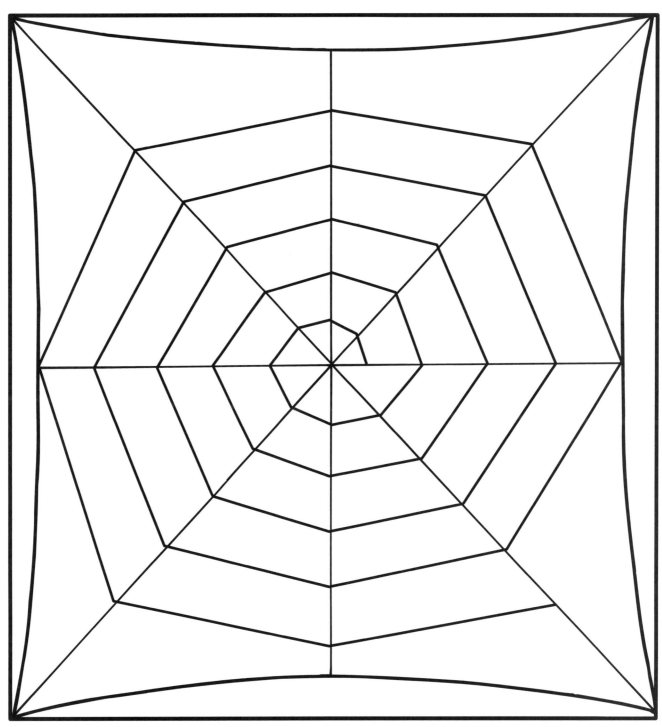

Spider Hunt

Materials

Collection of containers
Hand lenses
Spray bottles of water
Drawing paper
Crayons

Teacher's Notes

- It is always preferable to observe a creature in its natural habitat. Spiders can usually be found in shrubbery, particularly evergreen varieties. If this environment is not available near your classroom, catch some spiders ahead of time and keep them in covered jars or commercial "bug cages." After the children have had observation time, take the spiders back outside and release them.
- Gather the materials and prepare and display the center poster.
- Be sure there is a grown-up available to supervise the children when they are outside looking for spiders.

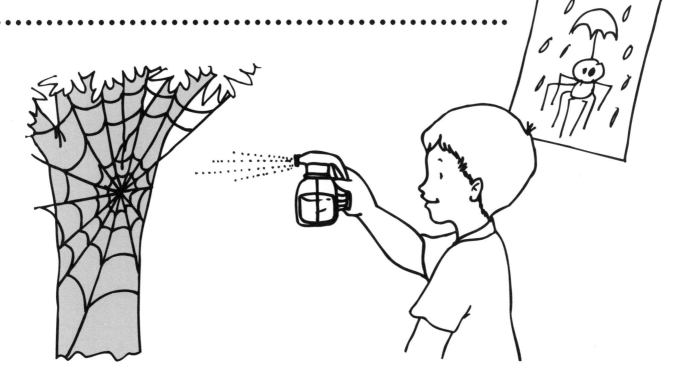

Spider Hunt

1. Go on a spider hunt.

2. If you find a web, spray it gently with water.

3. Did the spider come out? Talk with a friend about what happened.

4. Use the hand lens to look at the spider and its web.

5. Come in and make a picture and write about what you saw.

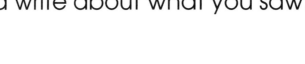

The Spider

Materials

Assembled student readers
Crayons
Silver glitter
White glue
Tagboard copies of the little Pointer Pal
    pattern, 1 per student
Strips of tagboard
Cellophane tape
Narrow-tip colored felt pens (for Pointer Pals)
Lengths of narrow ribbon, 1 per student
Scissors

Teacher's Notes for Student Readers

• Make copies of the student readers and assemble one per child.
  See directions for assembling in the Introduction.
• Show the children which pages to color (only two per day).

Special Touch: After the children have colored page 6 in their
student reader, have them glue a line of silver glitter on the spider's
web pictured there.

Notes for Pointer Pals

• After the children have completed their readers, put the materials
  for making the Pointer Pals in the Reading Center and show the
  children how to color and cut them out.
• Have an adult volunteer complete the students' Pointer Pals as
  described in the Introduction.

Pointer Pal Patterns ➡

The Spider

The spider crawled...

1.

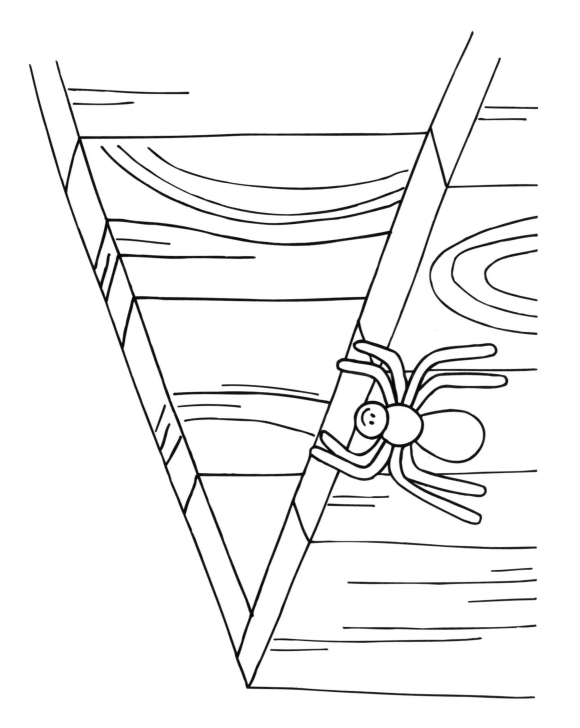

over the fence,

2.

across the yard.

3.

around the puddle.

4.

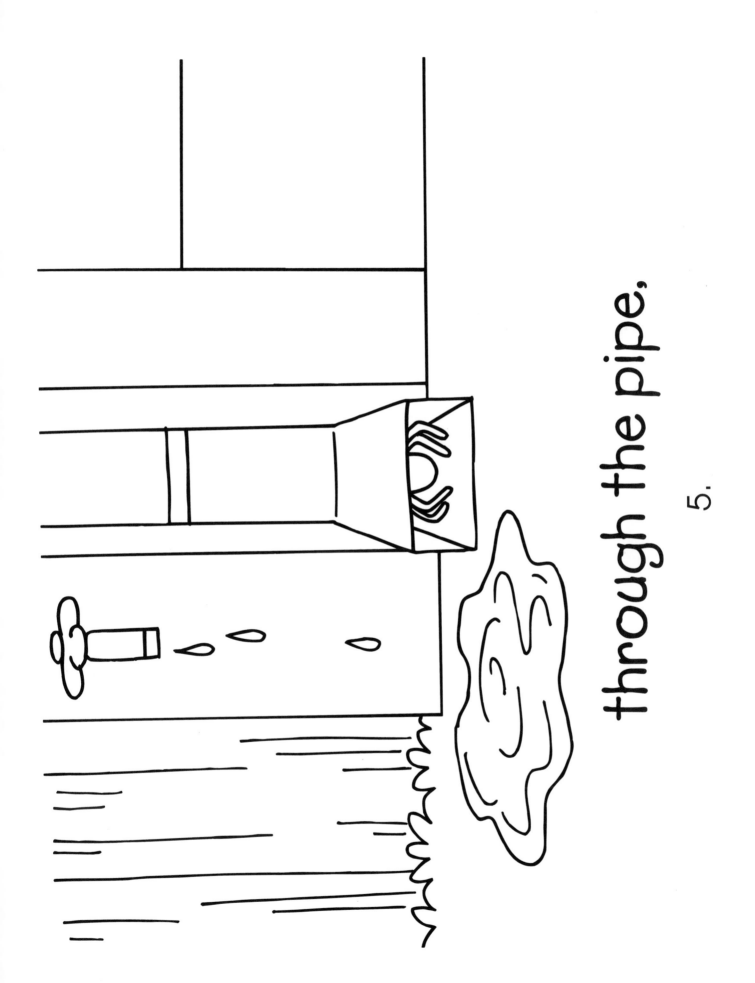

through the pipe.

5.

onto her web.

6.

just in time for dinner.

7.

The Spider

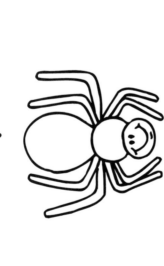

The spider crawled...

1.

across the yard.

3.

over the fence.

2.

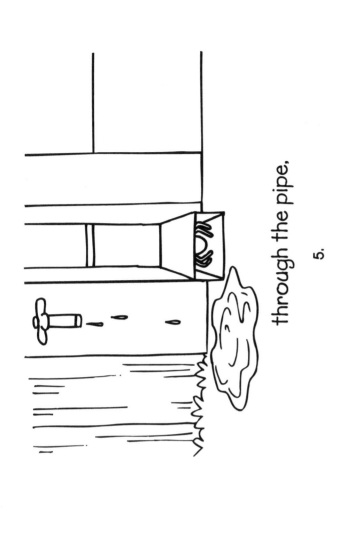

through the pipe.

5.

just in time for dinner.

7.

around the puddle.

4.

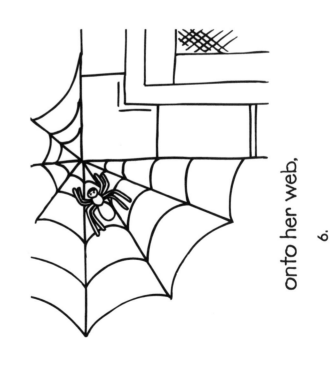

onto her web.

6.

TREES AND LEAVES

Circle Time

Start the Trees and Leaves theme studies by going for a walk with the children to select a tree to adopt. Discuss what the word "adoption" means before going. Bring along pencils, peeled crayons, plain paper, cardboard drawing boards, string, scissors, and one or two grocery bags for materials the children collect.

After the selection has been made, help the children gather data:

- Have several children hug the tree. Ask, "Can anyone wrap his or her arms all the way around our tree?" Select a child to help wrap a piece of string around the tree and cut it to the length of the trunk's circumference.
- Encourage the children to guess the number of branches on their tree. Try counting them together.
- Give the children paper and peeled crayons and show them how to do bark rubbings.
- Collect leaves, seeds, nuts, pods, and twigs that have fallen from the tree.
- Find a place for the children to sit at a short distance from the tree. Give them pencils, paper, and drawing boards, and have them draw the tree, including the parts that have been discussed.
- When you return to the classroom, have the children help you make a collage of the bark rubbings, drawings, and some of the leaves, pods, twigs, etc., that were gathered from around your adopted tree.

Explain the center activities.

 Book List

A Busy Year by Leo Lionni (Alfred A. Knopf, 1992).
Have You Seen Trees? by Joanne Oppenheim (Scholastic, 1967).
Red Leaf, Yellow Leaf by Lois Ehlert (Harcourt, Brace, 1991).
Someday a Tree by Eve Bunting (Houghton Mifflin, 1993).
A Tree Is Nice by Janice Udry (Harper and Row, 1956).

A Tree Is Nice

Materials

Listening post and earphones
Tape recorder and blank cassette
    recording tape
At least one copy of the book
    A Tree Is Nice by Janice Udry
Drawing paper and crayons

Teacher's Notes

- Tape the story. Gather the materials.
- Tell the children that after they have listened to the taped story they will make a picture of why they think trees are nice.
- Encourage them to write about their reason or dictate it to a helper to write down.
- When all of the children have been to the center, bind all the pictures they drew into a book for the classroom library.

A tree is nice because it gives us shade.

A tree is nice because it is a home for birds.

A tree is nice to decorate at Christmas.

A Tree Is Nice

A tree is nice because it

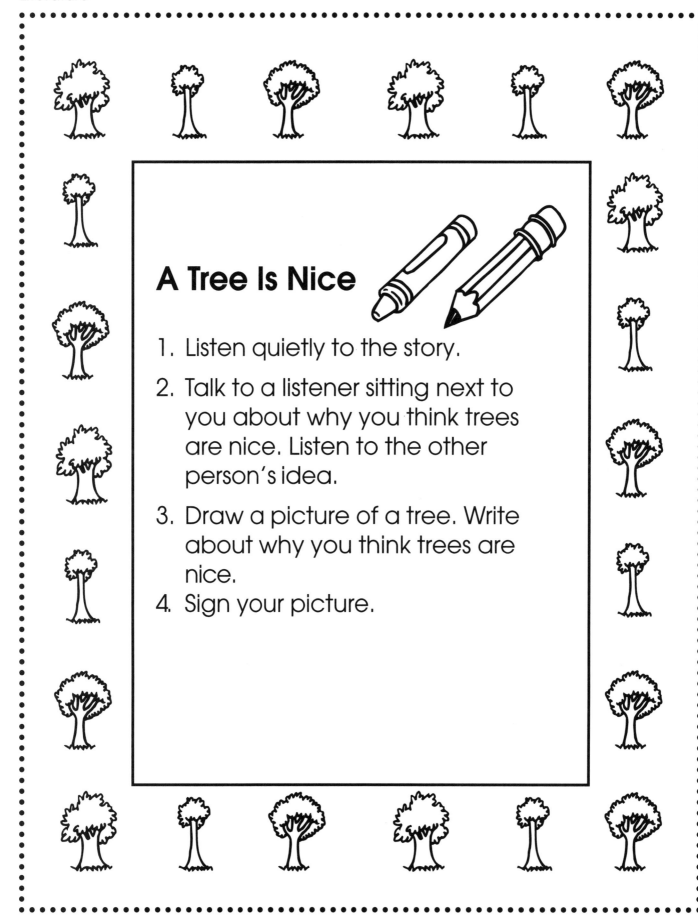

A Tree Is Nice

1. Listen quietly to the story.

2. Talk to a listener sitting next to you about why you think trees are nice. Listen to the other person's idea.

3. Draw a picture of a tree. Write about why you think trees are nice.

4. Sign your picture.

Autumn Leaves

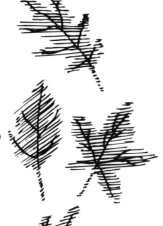

Materials

Fresh, pliable leaves in a variety of shapes
 and sizes
Tempera paint in autumn colors (red, orange,
 yellow, brown)
Paintbrushes
Dark brown construction paper, 12" x 18"
Large sheets of orange construction paper
Newspaper and paint shirts
Glue

Teacher's Notes

- Cover the work table with newspaper. Be sure the children wear protective aprons or paint shirts for this activity. Provide a place for the finished art pieces to dry.
- Gather the materials. Prepare and display the center poster.
- Be sure to gather fresh leaves for the project each day.
- Have the children each lay a leaf on newspaper vein side up. Show them how to brush paint onto that side of the leaf, turn it over, and press the painted side down onto a piece of dark brown construction paper. Have them carefully pull the painted leaf away from the paper and repeat the process over and over. Have them use the same or a different leaf until the paper is a collage of leaf prints.
- When the paint is dry, mount these beautiful works of art on a slightly larger piece of orange construction paper and create a display of autumn colors on a classroom bulletin board.

Autumn Leaves

1. Put a paint shirt on.

2. Choose a leaf. Turn it vein side up and paint it all over.

3. Turn the leaf over. Carefully press the painted side down on a big piece of brown paper.

4. Paint another leaf the same way. Use a different color.

5. Turn this leaf over and press the painted side down on the same piece of brown paper. This is called "leaf printing."

6. Cover the brown paper with many leaf prints.

Number Trees

Materials

Copies of the number trees activity page
White glue
Scissors
Crayons
Stapler and staples
Construction paper

Teacher's Notes

- Make three to five copies of the number trees activity page for each child, depending on the level of number understanding that has been reached.
- Gather the materials and prepare and display the center poster.
- Review number order and numeral formation with the children. Then demonstrate each step of the activity. Make a sample number tree to display in the center.

81

Number Trees

1. Cut each tree page along the line. Staple the pages together to make a book.
2. On the first page write the numeral 1 in the sign on the tree trunk.
3. On the second page write the numeral 2 in the sign on the tree.
4. Turn the pages one at a time and write the next numeral on each page.
5. Think of things that grow on trees (apples, oranges, lemons, nuts, peaches, cherries).
6. Draw one of the things on the first tree. Draw a set of two other things on the second tree. Draw a set of three other things on the third tree, and so on until you have a set of things that matches the numeral on each tree.
7. Color the trees.
8. Make a cover for your book. Write...

**My Number Tree Book
by _____**

Write your name here.

Number Trees

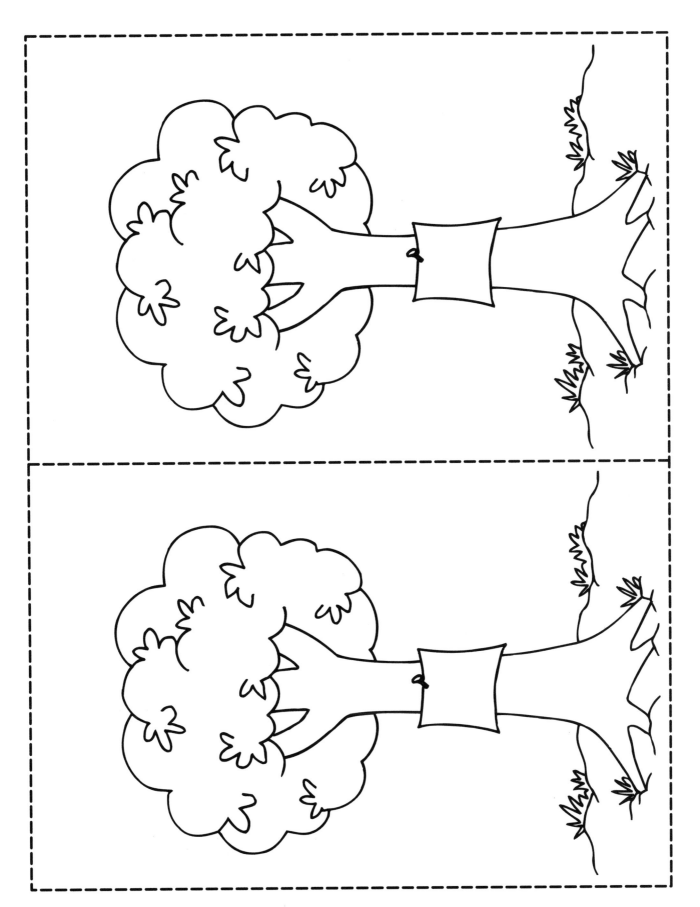

Leaf Rubbings

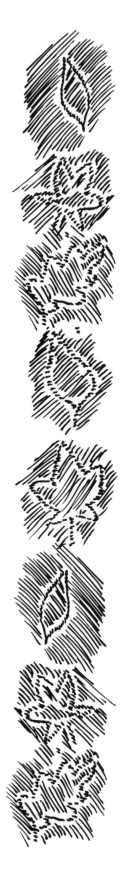

Materials

Paper lunch bags
Old newspapers
Peeled crayons in autumn colors (red, orange, yellow, brown)
Typing or copy paper
Hand lenses
Stapler
Cellophane tape

Teacher's Notes

- If there are deciduous trees near by, give the children collection bags and take them out each day before center time to gather leaves for this science center activity. Be sure the leaves are fresh and pliable and that you have a variety of shapes.
- Give each child a chance to look at the leaves with the hand lens. During group time have someone report about what he or she saw. Talk about the veins of a leaf.
- Gather the materials and prepare and display the center poster.
- Demonstrate each step for making the leaf rubbings:
  1. Choose a leaf and place it (vein side up) on top of several thicknesses of newspapers.
  2. Roll a small piece of tape, sticky side out, and place it under the leaf to hold it in place.
  3. Place a sheet of copy paper over the leaf to hold the paper in place. Tape the corners.
  4. Rub the side of a crayon across the entire paper until the whole leaf shape appears. Display this rubbing in the center.

Leaf Rubbings

1. Go on a leaf hunt. Try to find many different shapes. Put them in a bag.
2. Look at a leaf with a hand lens. Remember what you see to tell the class.
3. Tape one leaf on top of a "pad" of newspaper.
4. Cover the leaf with white paper and tape the corners of that paper down.
5. Rub over the whole leaf with the side of a crayon until the shape of the leaf appears on the paper.
6. Take a different leaf and make a rubbing on a new piece of paper.
7. Make three or four more rubbings.
8. Staple your pages together to make a leaf book.

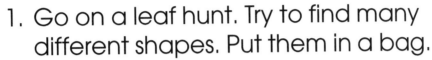
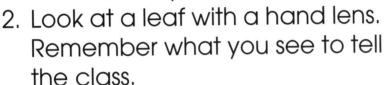

Leaves Are Falling

Materials

Assembled student readers
Crayons
Small pieces of construction paper in autumn colors
White glue
Tagboard copies of the little Pointer Pal pattern, 1 per child
Strips of tagboard
Cellophane tape
Narrow-tip colored felt pens for Pointer Pals
Scissors
Lengths of narrow ribbon, 1 per student

Teacher's Notes for Student Readers

• See the directions for assembling the student readers in the Introduction. Make one copy per child.
• Show the children which two pages to color each day.

Special Touch: Have the children color the leaves on the tree on page 1 of their readers. Then have them tear autumn-colored construction paper into very small scraps and glue them on the picture as though they were leaves falling to the ground.

Notes for Pointer Pals

• After the children have completed their readers, put the materials for making the Pointer Pals in the center and show them how to color and cut them out.
• Have an adult volunteer complete the students' Pointer Pals as described in the Introduction.

Pointer Pal Patterns ➧

Leaves Are Falling

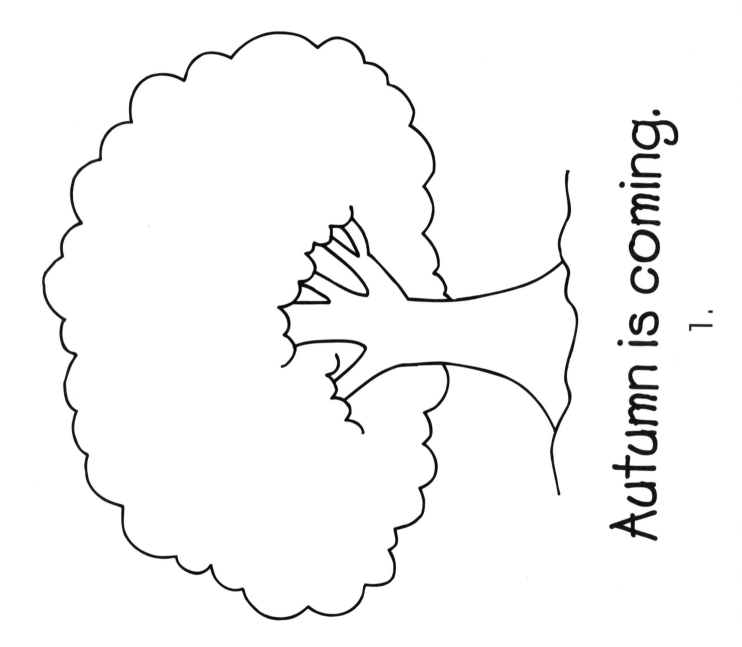

Autumn is coming.

1.

Red leaves are falling.

2.

Yellow leaves are falling.

3.

Orange leaves are falling.

4.

Brown leaves are falling.

5.

Red, yellow, orange, and brown
leaves are falling.

6.

 Center Connections ©1998 Monday Morning Books, Inc.

Winter is coming.

7.

Leaves Are Falling

Autumn is coming.

1.

Yellow leaves are falling.

3.

Red leaves are falling.

2.

Brown leaves are falling.

5.

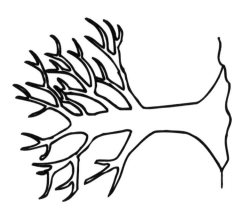

Winter is coming.

7.

Orange leaves are falling.

4.

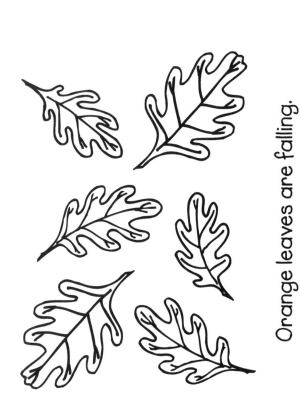

Red, yellow, orange,
and brown leaves are falling.

6.

WINTER

Discuss signs of winter that the children notice. Ask what the trees look like and what the weather conditions are like in the winter.

Mural

Use blue butcher paper for the background. Glue gentle hills cut from white butcher paper along the bottom. Have the children sponge-paint snowflakes onto the blue sky, and make snowmen and pictures of themselves playing in the snow to cut out and glue onto the background.

Poetry Poster

Make a copy of the poem "The Three Little Kittens" on chart paper and mount it at the children's eye level on a classroom wall. Have each child trace and cut out two mitten shapes and draw identical designs on each to resemble pairs of mittens. Staple a six-inch length of yarn between them and arrange them around the poetry poster.

Playhouse Transformations

Change the playhouse into a toy store for <u>December</u>. Ask the children to lend some of their old toys to "stock" in it. Gather some toys from the classroom shelves as well. The children may even be able to make some simple toys to include. Have the children make price tags, advertising posters, and signs. Remember to make play money available as well.

A ski lodge would be a great <u>January</u> playhouse transformation. Provide a cardboard carton with an opening cut from the bottom for the children to paint to look like a fireplace. Roll brown construction paper into logs and arrange them in the fireplace with crumpled orange and yellow tissue paper on top to resemble a roaring fire. Fill the dress-up box full of scarves, mittens, and ski hats.

Transform the playhouse in <u>February</u> into a post office where the children can mail the valentines they make. The office clerks will need counter space and some stamps, a little kitchen scale, pencils, a rubber stamp of some kind, and an ink pad. Have the children paint a box with a letter-size slit in it to look like an official mailbox. There they can mail their letters after buying their stamps.

WEATHER

Circle Time

Make a class list with the children of all the weather words they can think of. Draw a picture next to each word to help the beginning readers identify the words. Have the children illustrate and label their favorite weather type, and mount their pictures on the wall around the weather-word list.

Explain the center activities.

Book List

Bringing the Rain to Kapiti Plain by Verna Aardema (Dial Books, 1981).

Cloudy with a Chance of Meatballs by Judi Barrett (Macmillan, 1978).

Hurricane by David Wiesner (Houghton Mifflin, 1990).

It Looked Like Spilt Milk by Charles G. Shaw (Trophy Edition, 1988).

Katy and the Big Snow by Virginia Lee Burton (Houghton Mifflin, 1971).

Little Cloud by Eric Carle (Philomel Books, 1996).

Rain by Peter Spier (Doubleday, 1982).

Snowballs by Lois Elhert (Harcourt, Brace, 1995).

The Snowy Day by Ezra Jack Keats (The Viking Press, 1962).

The Storm Book by Charlotte Zolotow (Harper and Row, 1952).

The Sun, the Wind, and the Rain by Lisa Wextberg Peters (Henry Holt, 1988).

Thunder Cake by Patricia Polacco (Philomel, 1990).

Umbrella by Taro Yashima (Puffin Books, 1958).

Cloudy with a Chance of Meatballs

Materials

At least one copy of the book *Cloudy with a Chance of Meatballs*
Listening post and earphones
Tape recorder and blank cassette tape
Drawing paper and crayons

Teacher's Notes

• Tape the story and gather the materials.
• Prepare and display the center poster.
• Tell the children that this is a funny story and to listen carefully.
  Then when it is finished they can talk to another listener about
  the parts that were the funniest.

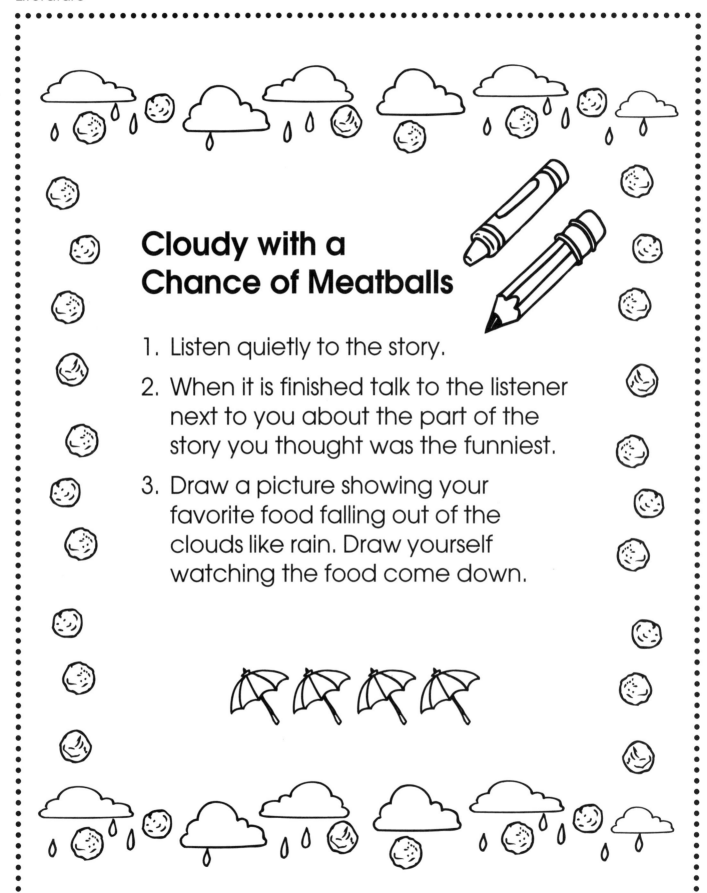

Cloudy with a Chance of Meatballs

1. Listen quietly to the story.

2. When it is finished talk to the listener next to you about the part of the story you thought was the funniest.

3. Draw a picture showing your favorite food falling out of the clouds like rain. Draw yourself watching the food come down.

Walking in the Rain

Materials

Umbrella pattern
Light blue construction paper
White construction paper
Colored felt-tip markers
Silver glitter
White glue
Waxed paper
Toothpicks
Scissors

Teacher's Notes

• Reproduce the umbrella pattern onto white construction paper, one per child.
• Cut the waxed paper into 3" x 3" squares.
• Gather the materials together and prepare and display the center poster.
• Show the children the designs on the umbrellas pictured on the poster. Encourage them to be creative as they color their umbrellas.
• Demonstrate each step of the activity. Make a sample to display in the center.

Walking in the Rain

1. Use the markers to design a beautiful umbrella.

2. Cut it out and glue it in the middle of a piece of blue paper.

3. Look at the pictures on this poster. Draw some legs on your umbrella like the ones you see on the poster. Draw some grass for the legs to stand on.

4. Put a puddle of white glue on a piece of waxed paper. Dip a toothpick into the glue and draw diagonal lines across your picture. Sprinkle the lines with silver glitter.

5. When the glue dries, shake the glitter onto a sheet of paper. Pour the glitter back into its bottle to recycle it.

Umbrella Pattern

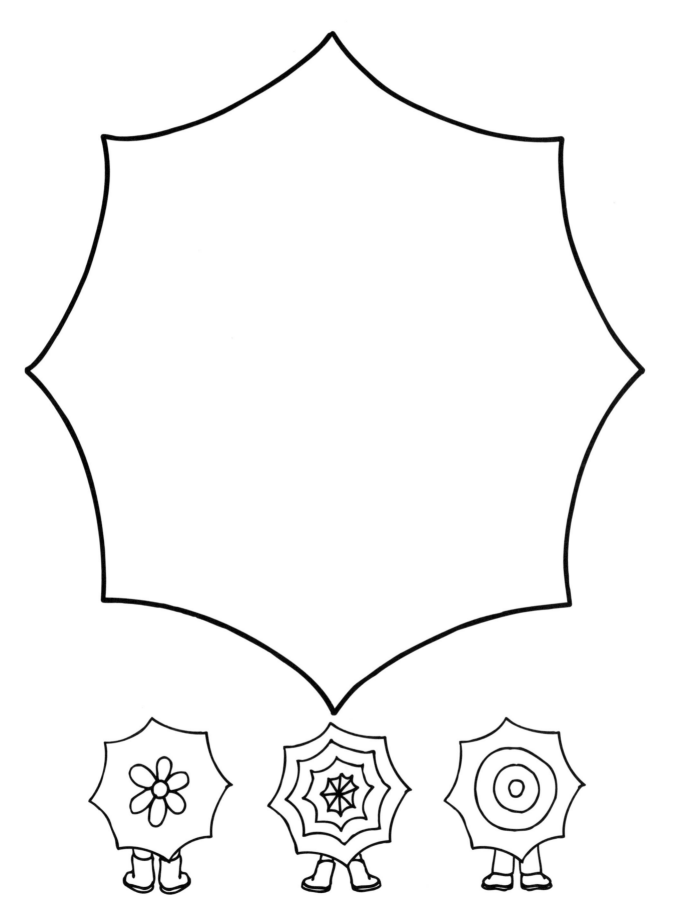

How Many Snowballs?

Materials

Cotton balls
Snowman activity page
9" x 12" pieces of tagboard
White glue
Crayons
Pencils

Teacher's Notes

- Make one copy of the snowman activity page for each student. Use tagboard.
- Gather the materials. Prepare and display the center poster.
- Demonstrate how to fill in a snowman shape with one layer of cotton balls.
- Draw an example and model the activity, showing the children how to do each step. Display the example in the center.

How Many Snowballs?

1. Color the worksheet.

2. Tell a friend how many snowballs (cotton balls) you think it will take to fill up the first snowman shape.

3. Fill in the first snowman shape with snowballs. Glue them down.

4. Count the snowballs you used. Write the number under the snowman.

5. Do the same thing for each snowman.

6. Ask a friend how many snowballs she or he used for each snowman.

7. Did you have the same or different numbers? Talk about it.

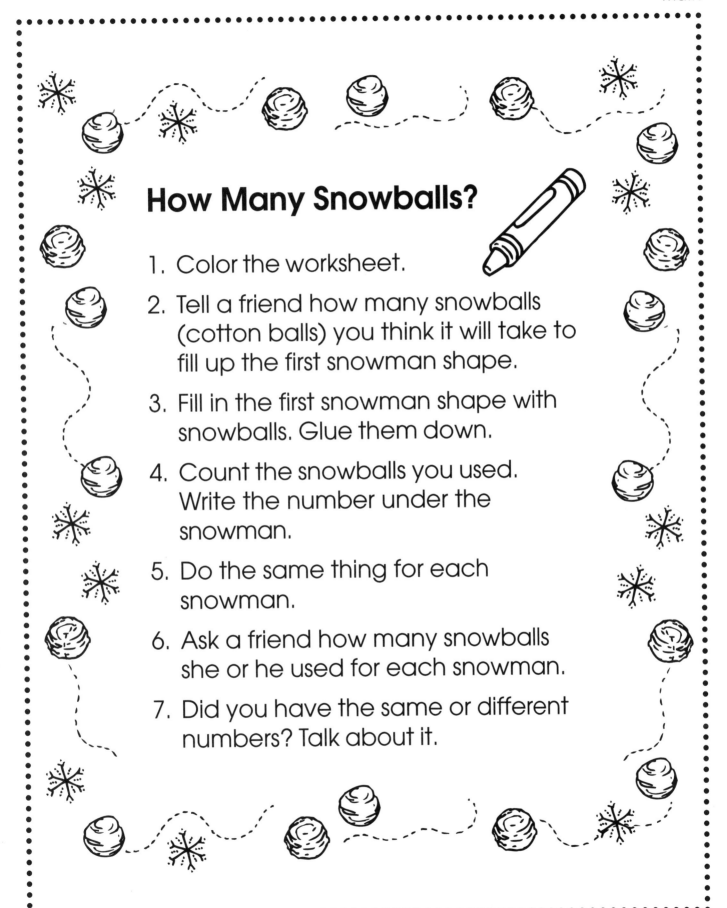

How Many Snowballs?

What Will I Wear?

Materials

Newsprint
Colored construction paper
Crayons
Pencils
Stapler and staples

Teacher's Notes

- Each child needs four pages and two pieces of colored construction paper.
- Gather the materials and prepare and display the center poster.
- Demonstrate the activity. Put the sample in the center.
- Plan to help some of the children assemble their books.

What Will I Wear?

Make a four-page book:

1. On one page draw yourself on a sunny, hot day. Draw the sun in the sky. Write "Hot Day."

2. On the next page draw yourself on a cool day. Color the sky blue. Write "Cool Day."

3. On another page draw yourself on a rainy day. Draw raindrops falling. Write "Rainy Day."

4. On the last page draw yourself on a snowy day. Draw snowflakes all around you. Write "Snowy Day."

5. Make a cover for your book. Write "What Will I Wear?" on the front.

6. Staple the book together.

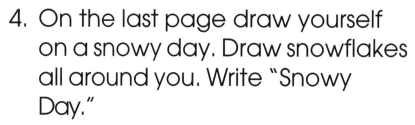

All Kinds of Weather

Materials

Assembled student readers
Crayons
Gold glitter
White glue
Tagboard copies of the little Pointer Pal
    pattern, 1 per child
Strips of tagboard
Cellophane tape
Narrow-tip colored felt pens for Pointer Pals
Scissors
Lengths of narrow ribbon, 1 per student

Teacher's Notes for Student Readers

• See the directions for assembling the student readers in the
  Introduction. Make one copy per child.
• Show the children which two pages to color each day.

<u>Special Touch</u>: When the children have finished coloring their
readers, let them glue gold glitter onto the lightning bolt on page 7.
Remind them to leave the book open at that page to allow the glue
to dry.

Notes for Pointer Pals

• After the children have completed their readers, put the materials
  for making the Pointer Pals in the center and show them how to
  color and cut them out.
• Have an adult volunteer complete the students' Pointer Pals as
  described in the Introduction.

Pointer Pal Patterns ▥➡

All Kinds of Weather

I can have fun in all kinds of weather.

1.

I can go swimming in sunny weather.

2.

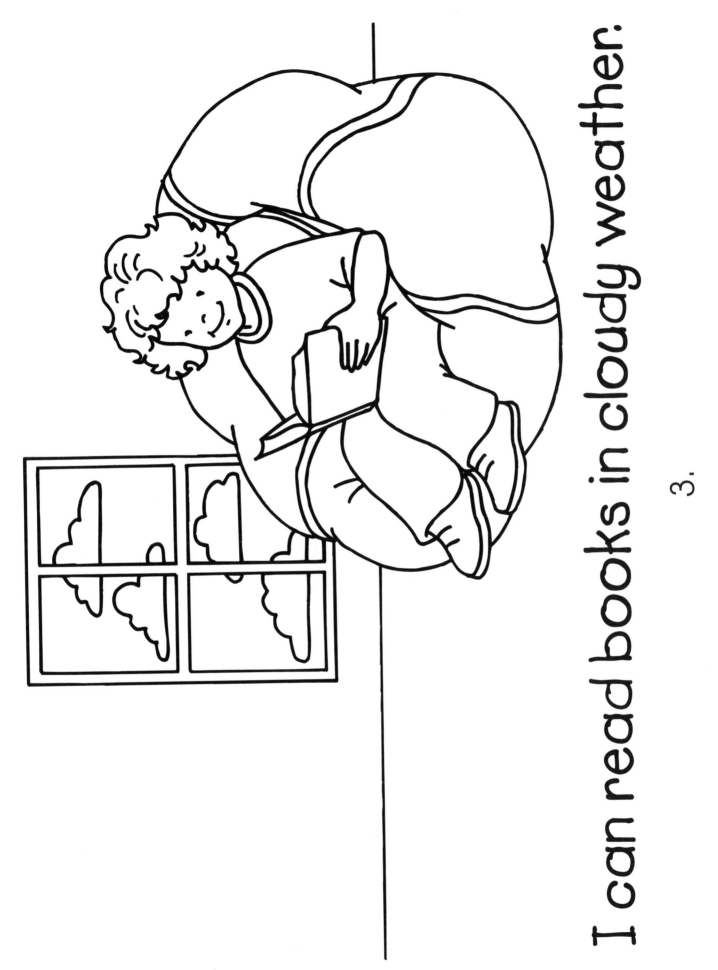

I can read books in cloudy weather.

3.

I can jump puddles in rainy weather.

4.

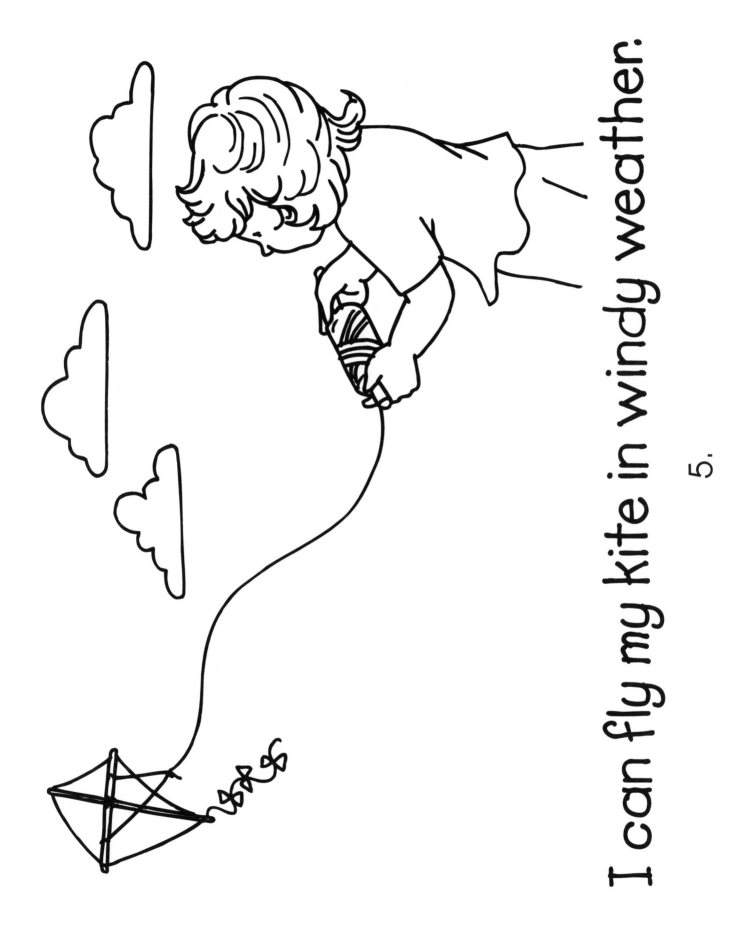

I can fly my kite in windy weather.

5.

I can build a snowman
in snowy weather.

6.

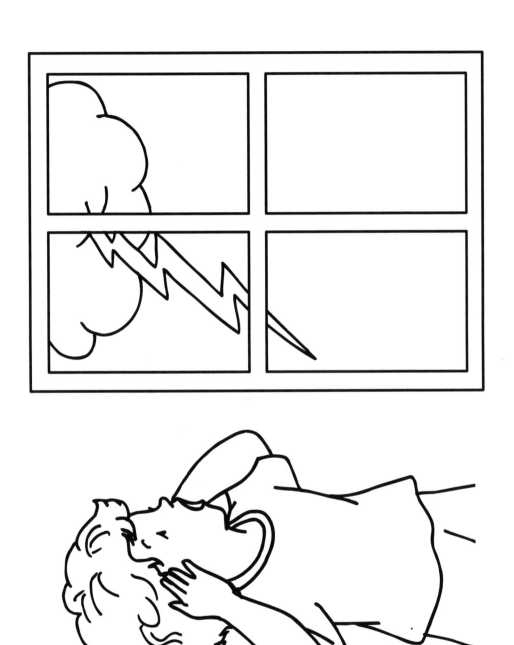

Wrong! I don't have fun in all kinds of weather.

7.

I have fun in all kinds of weather.

1.

I can read books in cloudy weather.

3.

All Kinds of Weather

I can go swimming in sunny weather.

2.

I can fly my kite in windy weather.

5.

Wrong! I don't have fun in all kinds of weather.

7.

I can jump puddles in rainy weather.

4.

I can build a snowman in snowy weather.

6.

119

CLOTHING

Circle Time

Ask the children to name items of clothing (shoes, skirts, pants, dresses, sweaters, belts, hats, etc.). Make a list of the things that are named. If possible, draw a sketch of each thing next to the word.

Play the game "What Are You Wearing":

Teacher chants—
    Are you wearing a _____? (Name an item of clothing.)
    Are you wearing a _____? (Name the same item.)
    Are you wearing a _____ (Name the same item again.) today?
Children who are wearing the clothing item named stand up and respond—
    Yes, I'm wearing a _____ . (Name the item of clothing.)
    Yes, I'm wearing a _____ . (Name the same item.)
    Yes, I'm wearing a _____ (Name the same item again.) today.
Vary the activity by adding different attributes to the chant question, such as, "Are you wearing black shoes?" or "Are you wearing short sleeves?"

Explain the center activities to the children.

 ## Book List

Charlie Needs a Cloak by Tomi de Paola (Prentice-Hall, 1982).
The Elves and the Shoemaker by Paul Galdone
    (Houghton Mifflin, 1984).
The Emperor's New Clothes retold by Ruth Belov Gross
    (Scholastic, 1977).
Froggy Gets Dressed by Jonathan London
    (Penguin Books, 1992).
Jesse Bear, What Will You Wear? by Nancy White Carlstrom
    (Macmillan, 1986).
Mary Wore Her Red Dress by Merle Peek (Clarion Books, 1992).
Shoes from Grandpa by Mem Fox (Orchard Books, 1989).

The Elves and the Shoemaker

Materials

Listening post and earphones
Cassette tape recorder and blank
  cassette tape
At least one copy of *The Elves and the
Shoemaker* by Paul Galdone
Drawing paper and crayons
Center poster

Teacher's Notes

• Tape the story. Gather the materials.
• Explain to the children that in this story the shoemaker and his
  wife give gifts of clothing to the little elves, who have none. Tell
  them that after they have listened to the story to think of what
  clothing they might give to someone in need and draw a picture
  about it.
• Prepare and display the center poster.

The Elves and the Shoemaker

1. Listen quietly to the story.

2. Talk to the listener sitting next to you about what kind of clothing you would give to someone in need.

3. Draw a picture about what you would give. Write or tell a story about it.

4. Put your name on your picture.

Paper Dolls

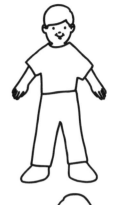

Materials

Paper dolls activity page
White copy paper
Crayons
Pencils
Scissors
Plastic bags, 1 per child
Oak tag

Teacher's Notes

• Gather the materials and prepare and display the center poster.
• Make copies of the paper dolls activity page, one or two per child.
• Many children know nothing about the commercial paper dolls of past generations. Make up samples to display in the center.
• Explain each step as you demonstrate the technique of using the paper doll as a pattern for making the clothes. Be sure to show the children how to draw rectangular tabs on the clothing at the shoulders and the waist to hold the clothes on the paper doll.

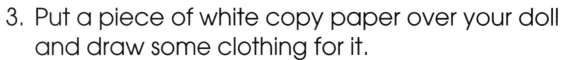

Paper Dolls

1. Choose a paper doll.
2. Color it and cut it out.
3. Put a piece of white copy paper over your doll and draw some clothing for it.

   • To make pants, trace the doll's hips and legs.
   • To make a shirt, trace the arms and upper body.
   • To make a dress, trace arms, upper body, and hips. Draw a line across the bottom of the dress.

4. Draw on collars, buttons, and belts.
5. Decorate and color the doll's clothing.
6. Draw rectangular tabs on the clothing's shoulders and waist to hold the clothes on.
7. Cut out the clothing. Fold the tabs back.
8. Put the clothing you have made on the doll.

Paper Dolls

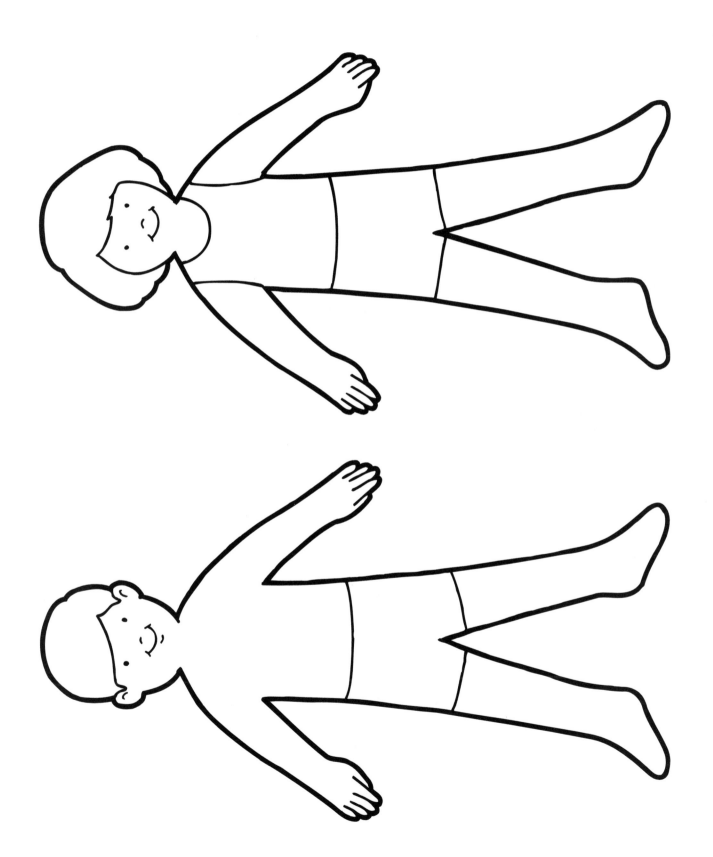

Designer Shirts

Materials

Wallpaper sample cards, 1 per child
White drawing paper (8" x 10"), 1 per child
8" x 10" pieces of oak tag, 1 per child
Crayons or colored felt markers
Oak tag shirt pattern, 1 per child
Scissors
Stapler

Teacher's Notes

• Search through wallpaper sample books to find designs composed of small repeating patterns that will be simple enough for the children to copy. Geometric patterns, plaids, and stripes are best.

• Make a wallpaper sample card for each child by placing a 4" by 10" piece of wallpaper on top of an 8" by 10" piece of oak tag. Staple the two together along one 10" side.

• Gather all the materials and prepare and display the center poster.

• During the introductory discussion of this activity, tell the children that the fabric our clothing is made from is often decorated with a repeating pattern. Point out some examples from the clothing they are wearing.

• Show the children how to use the wallpaper sample cards to create patterned "fabric" for a designer shirt. (See the center poster.) Make a sample to display at the center.

• Display the finished shirts in a class book or on a bulletin board, titled "Designer Shirts."

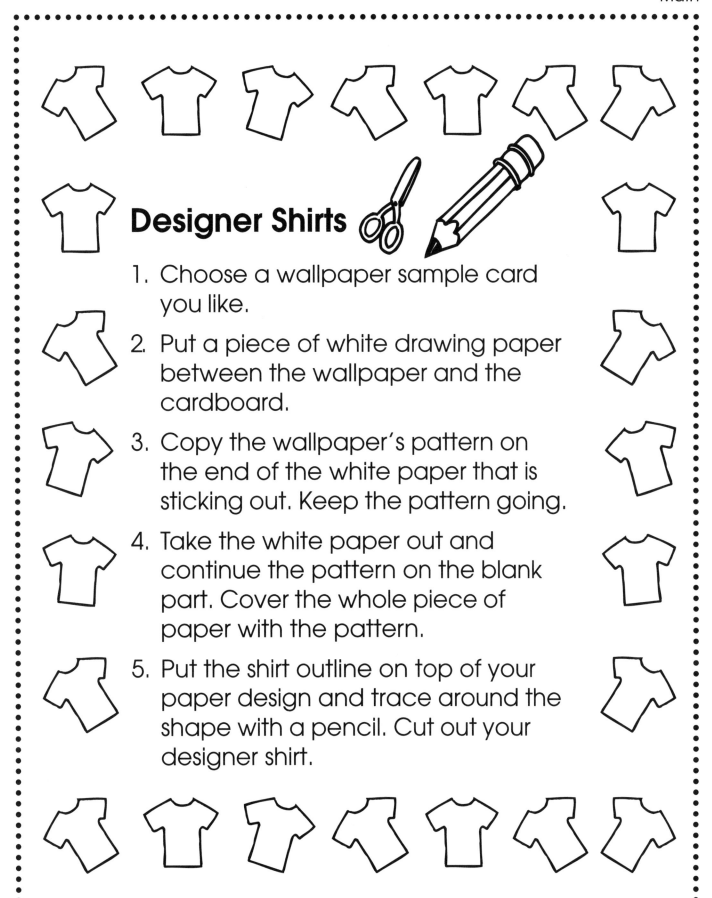

Designer Shirts

1. Choose a wallpaper sample card you like.

2. Put a piece of white drawing paper between the wallpaper and the cardboard.

3. Copy the wallpaper's pattern on the end of the white paper that is sticking out. Keep the pattern going.

4. Take the white paper out and continue the pattern on the blank part. Cover the whole piece of paper with the pattern.

5. Put the shirt outline on top of your paper design and trace around the shape with a pencil. Cut out your designer shirt.

Designer Shirts

What Are You Wearing?

Materials

Laundry basket
Variety of clothing suitable for all weather
   conditions in your area
4 Hula-Hoops or jump ropes
Weather condition signs
Scissors
Oak tag
Sticks or dowels
Glue
Colored markers

Teacher's Notes

• Send a note home with a list of appropriate clothing and ask
parents to contribute items they may have. Such a list could
include:

Rainy Day Clothing	**Hot Weather Clothing**
raincoats	swimsuits
ponchos	shorts
rain boots	sandals
	tank tops

Cold Day Clothing	**Mild Weather Clothing**
heavy jackets/coats	cotton dresses/shirts
mittens or gloves	sneakers
knit caps	lightweight sweaters

• Make a copy on oak tag of each of the four weather condition
signs. Cut them apart, then color and mount each on a stick.
Arrange the Hula-Hoops on the floor and display one of the posters
in each.
• Gather the other materials. Prepare and display the center poster.
• Discuss how the weather affects what we wear. Explain the
weather signs to the children. Show them a few of the items of
clothing and ask in what kind of weather each would be worn. Put
each item in the appropriate area.

What Are You Wearing?

1. Choose three friends to work with.

2. Work together to lay out four circles on the floor. Use Hula-Hoops or make jump rope circles.

3. Put a weather sign in each circle.

4. Take turns choosing something out of the clothing basket. Put each piece in the circle that tells in what kind of weather the clothing should be worn.

5. Continue taking turns until the basket is empty.

6. Talk about what you chose for each kind of weather. Did you all agree? If you did not agree, tell why.

Weather Condition Signs

Center Connections ©1998 Monday Morning Books, Inc.

Get Dressed, Little Bear!

Materials

Assembled student readers
Crayons
Old jeans or blue denim fabric
Thin white paper
White glue
Tagboard copies of the little Pointer Pal
    pattern, 1 per child
Strips of tagboard
Cellophane tape
Narrow-tip colored felt pens for Pointer Pals
Scissors
Lengths of narrow ribbon, 1 per student

Teacher's Notes for Student Readers

• See the directions for assembling the student readers in the Introduction. Make one reader per child.
• Show the children which two pages to color each day.

Special Touch: Cut out pants shapes (one per child) from old jeans fabric. Make a white paper pattern first by tracing the picture of Little Bear's pants on page 7. Show the children how to glue the denim pants to the picture of Little Bear's pants in their reader.

Notes for Pointer Pals

• After the children have completed their readers, put the materials for making the Pointer Pals in the center. Show the children how to color and cut them out.
• Have an adult volunteer complete the students' Pointer Pals as described in the Introduction.

Pointer Pal Patterns ⫸

"Get dressed, Little Bear!"

1.

Little Bear put on his shirt.

2.

Center Connections ©1998 Monday Morning Books, Inc.

Little Bear put on his socks and his shoes.

3.

Little Bear put on his jacket
and his hat.

4.

5.

6.

Center Connections ©1998 Monday Morning Books, Inc.

How embarrassing!

7.

140

"Get dressed, Little Bear!"

1.

Little Bear put on his socks and his shoes.

3.

Little Bear! Get dressed!

Little Bear put on his shirt.

2.

Center Connections ©1998 Monday Morning Books, Inc.

Little Bear! You forgot your pants!

5.

How embarrassing!

7.

Little Bear put on his jacket and his hat.

4.

Oops!

6.

HOMES

Circle Time

Discuss the different kinds of places that people and animals live in.
Make a chart, labeling one side "People Homes" and the other
"Animal Homes."

Record all the children's ideas in the appropriate columns.
For example:

People Homes	Animal Homes
houses	caves
apartments	trees
duplexes	seas
condominiums	dens
mobile homes	pens

Teach the children the following rhyme:
Here is a nest for the robin. *(Cup both hands.)*
Here is a hive for the bee. *(Put fists together.)*
Here is a hole for the bunny. *(Finger and thumb form a circle.)*
And here is a <u>*(have the children fill in the name of their dwelling*</u>)
for me. *(Fingertips together to make a roof.)*

Then explain the center activities.

 **Book List**

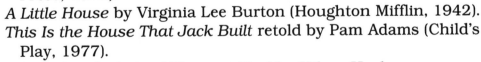

Animal Homes by Joyce Pope (Troll, 1994).
A Big Quiet House by Heather Forest (August House, 1996).
Big Red Barn by Margaret Wise Brown (Harper Collins, 1989).
A House Is a House for Me by Mary Ann Hoberman (Viking
    Press, 1978).
A Little House by Virginia Lee Burton (Houghton Mifflin, 1942).
This Is the House That Jack Built retold by Pam Adams (Child's
    Play, 1977).
What's Inside Animal Homes edited by Hilary Hockman
    (Dorling Kindersley, 1993).

The Little House

Materials

At least one copy of *A Little House*
  by Virginia Lee Burton
Listening post and earphones
Tape recorder and blank cassette tape
Drawing paper and crayons
Sentence strips, 1 per student

Teacher's Notes

• Tape the story and gather the materials.
• Explain to the children that after they listen to the story they will be making pictures of little houses for a class book. Ask them to imagine a special place for their house to be, such as beside a river or lake, in the forest, on a mountain, by the ocean, in the country or city, etc.
• Write the following sentence on several sentence strips for the children to copy on their drawings. Explain that they should put their own name on the line.

This is _____'s little house.

• Prepare and display the center poster. Make a model page for the center.

The Little House

1. Listen quietly to the story.

2. Talk to the listener sitting next to you about where you would like your house to be.

3. Draw a picture of a little house. Draw it in a place you would like to live.

4. Copy the sentence onto your picture. Write your name on your paper where the line is:

   This is _____ 's little house.

My Dream Home

Materials

Different kinds of paper in a variety of
  colors and sizes (construction paper,
  tissue, wallpaper, corrugated paper)
Cloth scraps
Buttons
Felt markers
White glue
Scissors

Teacher's Notes

- Lay out all the materials. Prepare and display the center poster.
- Have the children think of all the different kinds of homes there
  are. Suggest some others that they might not think of, such as log
  cabins, castles, caves, tree houses, igloos, tipis, etc. Make a list.
- Tell the children to make a cut-and-paste picture of a house they
  would like to live in for awhile. You may wish to discuss various
  cut-and-paste techniques, such as making doors that open, curtains at the windows, etc. The pictures are usually more creative,
  however, if the children implement their own ideas.
- Put the children's actual addresses on the completed dream
  homes and display them on a bulletin board.

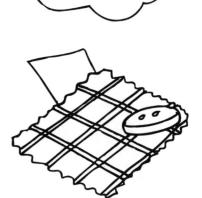

My Dream Home

1. Think of the kind of home you would like to live in.

2. Cut out its shape.

3. Add other things to your house to make it look like the home of your dreams.

   Ideas:
   windows
   doors
   curtains
   chimney
   drawbridge for a castle
   towers for a castle
   tunnel for an igloo
   tree for a tree house

Where Do You Live?

Materials

"Where Do You Live?" activity page
Pencils
Clipboards, 1 per child

Teacher's Notes

- Make a copy of the activity paper for each child.
- Explain the center activity and set out the materials.
- If the children have not been introduced to tallying, take time to show them how to do it.
- Be sure the children know the names of the kinds of houses pictured on the graph before they begin the activity.

Where Do You Live?

1. Fasten a copy of the home graph to your clipboard.

2. Ask someone which home is most like hers/his.

3. Make a tally mark under the picture chosen.

4. Ask at least 10 people and mark their answers.

5. Count up the tally marks.

6. Talk about your graph with someone. Ask such questions as:

   • Do more people live in houses than apartments?
   • In which kind of home do the fewest people live?
   • How many more people live in duplexes than in mobile homes?

Where Do You Live?

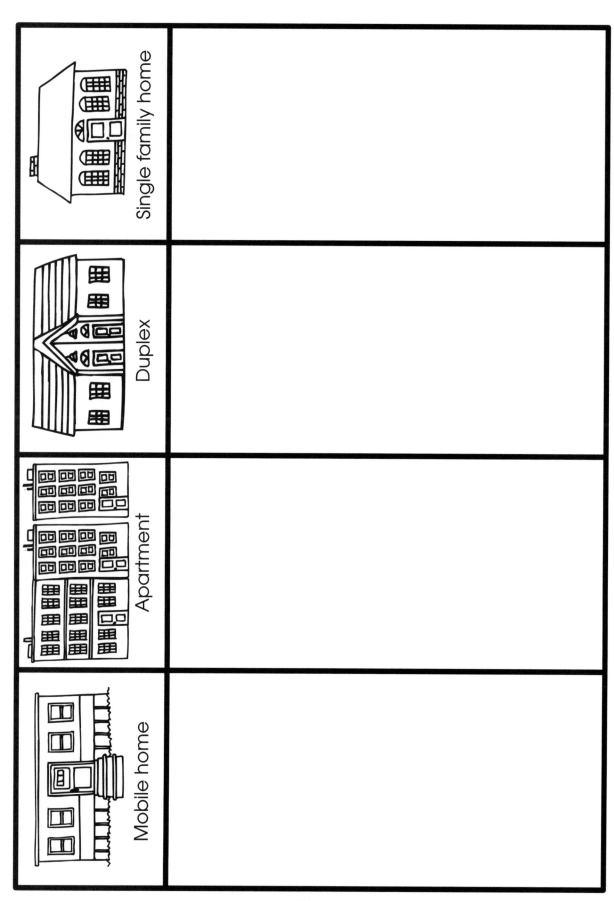

Home Free

Materials

"Home Free" game card activity page
9" x 12" pieces of lightweight cardboard,
   1 per child
Scissors
Small plastic bags, 1 per child

Teacher's Notes

- Gather the materials and prepare and display the center poster.
- Make copies of the game card page on lightweight cardboard, one for each child.
- Discuss animal homes with the children in preparation for this center's activities. Talk about where each of the animals pictured on the playing cards lives.

ants—anthills	horses—stables
bees—beehives	chickens—coops
whales—oceans	bears—dens
dogs—doghouses	

- Review the game of Memory with the children:
  — Shuffle the cards.
  — Spread them face down on the table.
  — One player turns two cards over for all to see.
  — If the cards match, that player wins the pair and plays again. If not, the cards are turned face down again and the next player takes a turn.
  — When all the cards have been matched, the player with the most pairs wins.

Home Free

1. Cut the game cards apart along the lines.

2. Ask a friend to play with you, or play by yourself.

3. Shuffle the game cards and lay them face down on the table or floor.

4. Let your friend turn two cards over for both of you to see. If they match, your friend wins the pair and takes another turn.

5. If the cards do not match, your friend turns them face down. Then you get to take a turn.

6. When all the cards have been matched, the player with the most pairs is the winner.

7. Put your cards in a plastic bag to take home to play.

 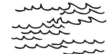

Home Free Game Cards

ants	den	ocean
squirrel	anthill	dog house
bee	dog	bear
pig	beehive	pen
whale	stable	horse
tree	chicken	coop

153

Is This Your Home?

Materials

Assembled student readers
Crayons
3" x 3" pieces of white drawing paper
White glue
Tagboard copies of the little Pointer Pal
    pattern, 1 per child
Strips of tagboard
Cellophane tape
Narrow-tip colored felt pens for Pointer Pals
Scissors
Lengths of narrow ribbon, 1 per student

Teacher's Notes for Student Readers

• See the directions for assembling the student readers in the
  Introduction. Make one reader per child.
• Show the children which two pages to color each day.

Special Touch: After the children have colored all the pages in
their readers, have them make a picture of their own homes on the
3" squares of drawing paper. Have them glue the picture above the
text on the last page of their books.

Notes for Pointer Pals

• After the children have completed their readers, put the materials
  for making the Pointer Pals in the center. Show the children how
  to color and cut them out.
• Have an adult volunteer complete the students' Pointer Pals as
  described in the Introduction.

Pointer Pal Patterns ▦➡

Is This Your Home?

Center Connections ©1998 Monday Morning Books, Inc.

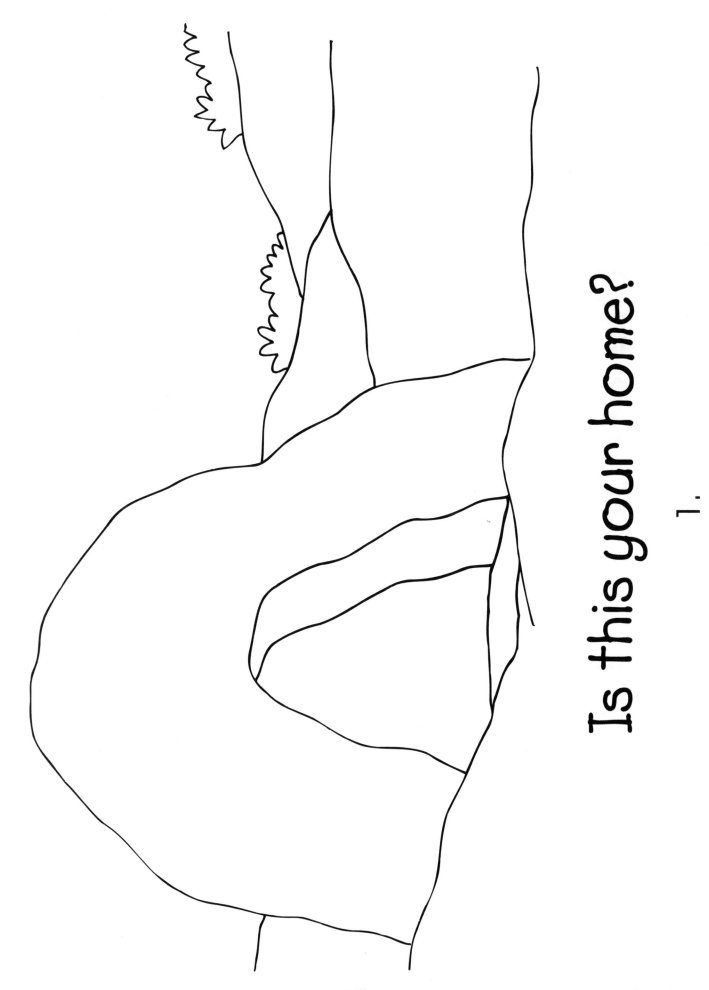

Is this your home?

1.

No, no, no!

This is the home of some foxes.

2.

Is this your home?

3.

No, no, no!

This is the home of some baby birds.

4.

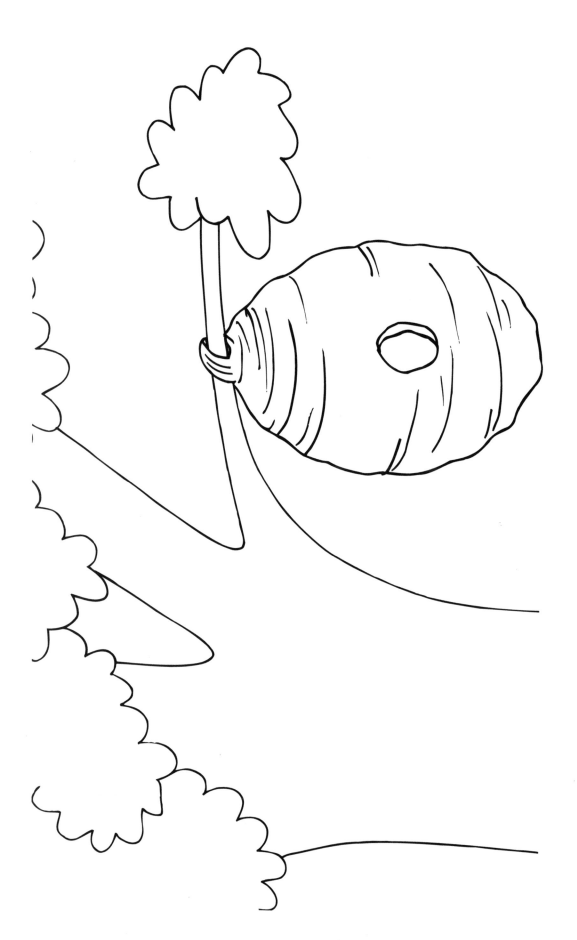

Is this your home?

5.

No, no, no!

This is the home of some bees.

6.

Is this your home?
Yes, yes, yes!
This is my home.

7.

Is This Your Home?

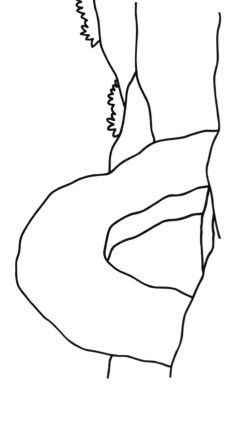

Is this your home?

1.

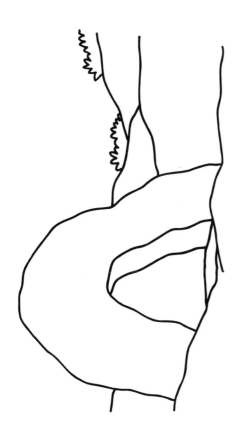

No, no, no!
This is the home of some foxes.

2.

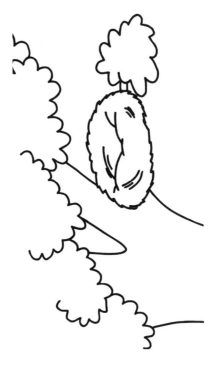

Is this your home?

3.

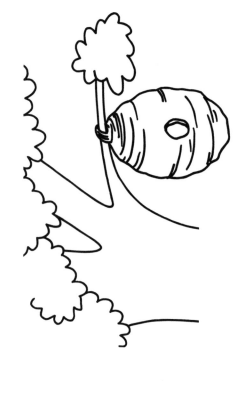

Is this your home?

5.

No, no, no!
This is the home of some baby birds.

4.

Is this your home?
Yes, yes, yes! This is my home.

7.

No, no, no!
This is the home of some bees.

6.

DAY AND NIGHT

Circle Time

Discuss day and night concepts with the children. Ask what night-time is and what daytime is. Ask what they see at each time and what they do. Talk about the sun and the moon.

Demonstrate the movement of the Earth as it relates to the sun. Choose a child to be the sun and give her/him a flashlight. Choose another child to be the Earth. Ask the "Earth" to turn around slowly while the "sun" shines the flashlight on him/her. Explain that sunlight shines on the Earth as it turns in space. Explain that it is daytime on the Earth in the area that is lit and that it is nighttime where it is dark. Also explain that even though an area on Earth is dark the sun is still in the sky.

Explain the center activities.

 **Book List**

Goodnight Moon by Margaret Wise Brown
   (Harper and Row, 1947).
Goodnight, Owl by Pat Hutchins (Houghton Mifflin, 1989).
Night Is Coming by W. Nikola-Lisa (Dutton Children's
   Books, 1991).
The Sun's Day by Mordicai Gerstein (Harper and Row, 1989).
Sun Up, Sun Down by Gail Gibbons (Harcourt, Brace,
   Jovanovich, 1983).
Time for Bed by Mem Fox (Harcourt, Brace, 1993).
Wait Til the Moon Is Full by Garth Williams
   (Harper Collins, 1948).

Goodnight Moon

Materials

At least one copy of *Goodnght Moon*
  by Margaret Wise Brown
Listening post and earphones
Cassette recorder and blank cassette tape
9" x 12" newsprint
Crayons and pencils
Stapler and staples

Teacher's Notes

• Tape the story and gather the materials.
• Staple four to six pieces of newsprint together to make a blank book for each child.
• Tell the children that after they have listened to the story they will make their own books about things in their bedrooms that they can say "Good night" to.
• Prepare and display the center poster.

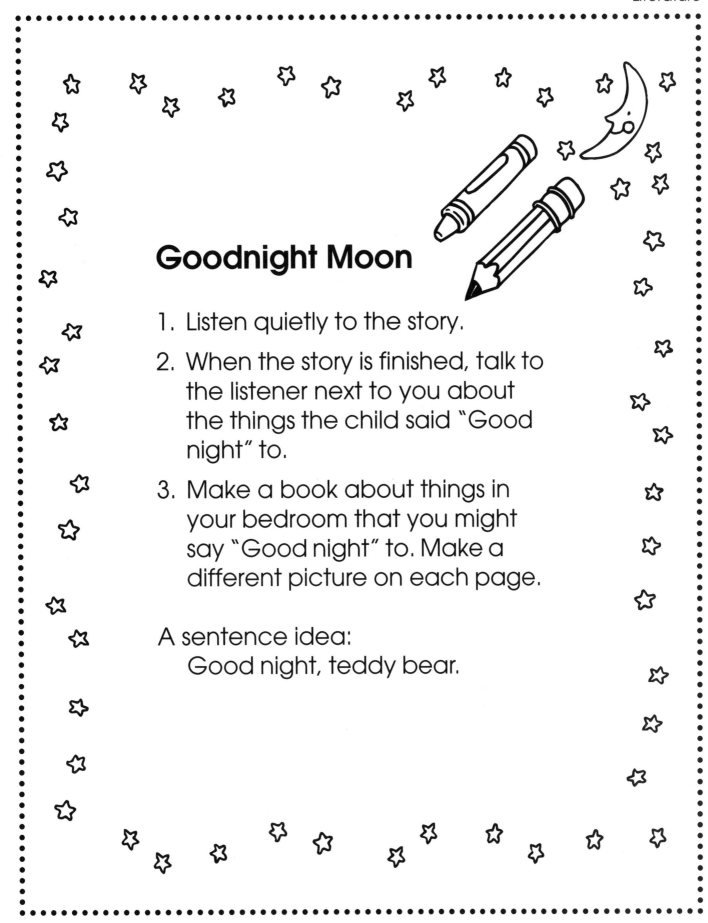

Goodnight Moon

1. Listen quietly to the story.

2. When the story is finished, talk to the listener next to you about the things the child said "Good night" to.

3. Make a book about things in your bedroom that you might say "Good night" to. Make a different picture on each page.

A sentence idea:
    Good night, teddy bear.

The Night Sky

Materials

White drawing paper
Crayons
Black watercolor paint
Watercolor brushes

Teacher's Notes

- Gather the materials and prepare and display the center poster.
- Tell the children to press down hard with their crayons as they make their pictures. In that way the color will resist the paint when it is applied.
- Model all the steps in the activity as an introduction to the center. Display the sample in the center.

The Night Sky

1. Along the bottom of your paper make some low hills. Color them green. Be sure you press down hard with your green crayon.

2. Make a picture of stars and the moon. Use a white and a yellow crayon. Press down very hard.

3. Cover your whole picture with black watercolor paint. It will look like the sky at night.

It's About Time

Materials

Paper
Lightweight card stock (oak tag)
Crayons
Brads
Scissors
Paste
Clock face and hands patterns
Sentence masters
Stapler

Teacher's Notes

• Prepare and display the center poster.
• Make a seven-page blank book for each child (5 $\frac{1}{2}$" x 8 $\frac{1}{2}$").
• Make one oak tag set per student of the clock face and hands patterns.
• Make one copy per child of the sentence masters.
• Demonstrate each step of the activity for the children. Make a sample to display in the center.

It's time to go to school!

It's time to get up.

It's time for lunch.

It's time for dinner.

It's About Time

1. Cut out the sentences. Put them in order and paste one on each page.

2. Make a picture on each page that goes with the sentence.

3. Color the clock page.

4. Cut out the two hands of the clock. Ask a grown-up to help you put them on the clock with a brad.

5. Staple your book onto the clock page under the clock.

6. Read the book. Show the time on the clock that goes with each page.

It's About Time

Good Night

It's About Time

It's time to get up!
It's time to go to school.
It's time for lunch.
It's time to go home.
It's time for dinner.
It's time for bed.

Center Connections ©1998 Monday Morning Books, Inc.

Sunlight Prints

Materials

Dark-colored construction paper
  (not fadeless—blue works very well)
Paper clips (varied sizes), old keys, pencils,
  other small objects with interesting shapes
Scissors
A sunny day

Teacher's Notes

• Gather the materials and prepare and display the center poster.
• Cut the construction paper into 4" x 4" squares.
• Model each step of the activity for the children. Display a sample
  in the center.

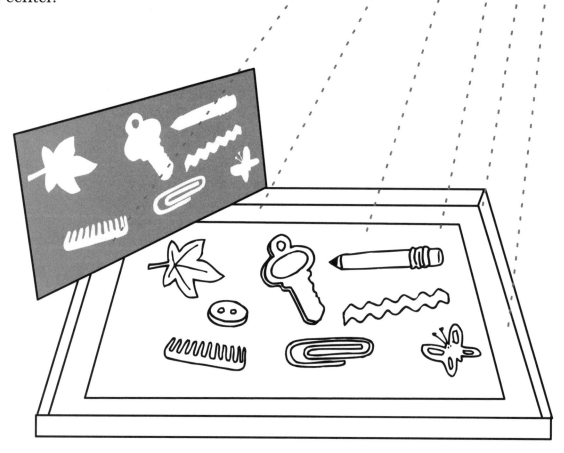

Sunlight Prints

1. Lay a piece of dark-colored paper in the sun.

2. Arrange some small things in a design on top of the paper.

3. Don't move the small objects or the paper.

4. When the paper and objects have been in the sun a long time, bring them inside. Take the objects off the paper.

5. Talk to a friend about what you see.

6. Hang your sunlight print on the wall.

Wake Up! Wake Up!

Materials

Assembled student readers
Crayons
Small gold and silver stick-on stars
Strips of tagboard
Cellophane tape
Narrow-tip colored felt pens for Pointer Pals
Scissors
Lengths of narrow ribbon, 1 per student

Teacher's Notes for Student Readers

- See the directions for assembling the student readers in the Introduction. Make one reader per child.
- Show the children which two pages to color each day.

Special Touch: Have the children color page 6 with either a black or a dark-blue crayon to depict the night sky. Give them some small silver and gold stick-on stars to press on the page after they have colored it.

Notes for Pointer Pals

- After the children have completed their readers, put the materials for making the Pointer Pals in the center. Show the children how to color and cut them out.
- Have an adult volunteer complete the students' Pointer Pals as described in the Introduction.

Pointer Pal Patterns ➡

Wake Up! Wake Up!

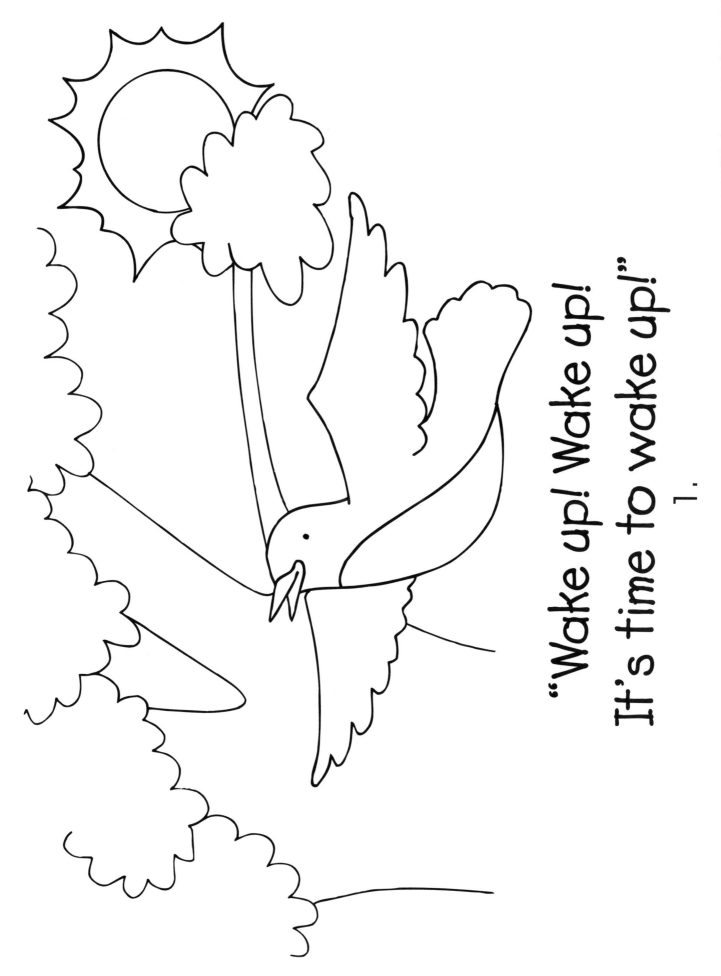

"Wake up! Wake up!
It's time to wake up!"

1.

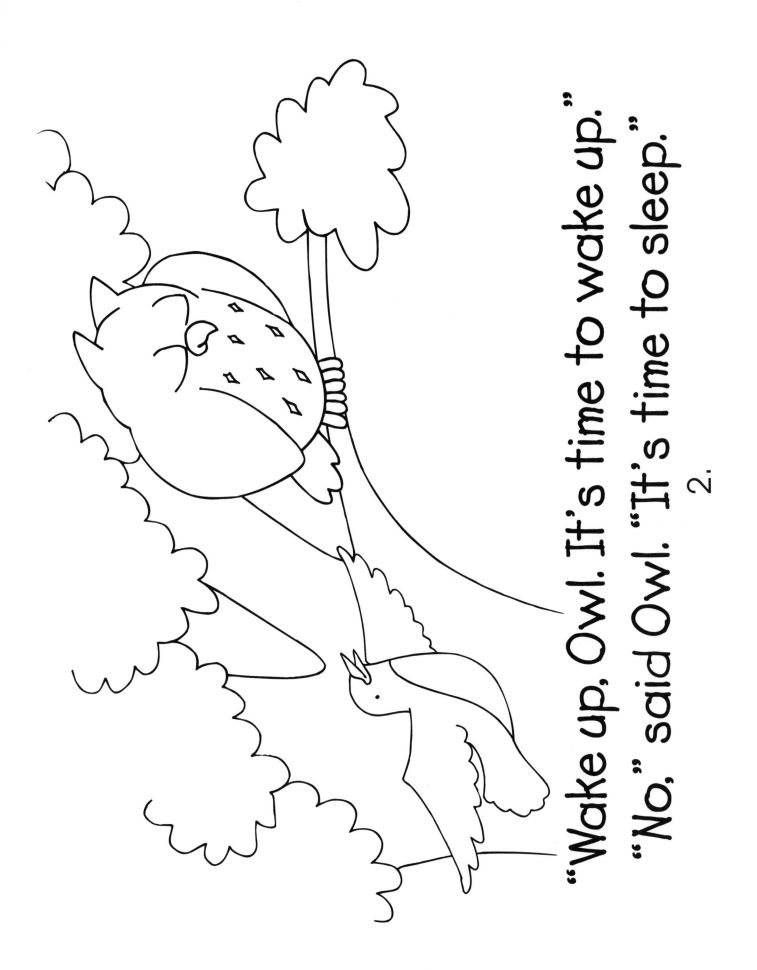

"Wake up, Owl. It's time to wake up."
"No," said Owl. "It's time to sleep."

2.

"Wake up, Bat. It's time to wake up."
"No," said Bat. "It's time to sleep."

3.

"Wake up, Raccoon. It's time to wake up."

"No," said Raccoon. "It's time to sleep."

4.

"Wake up, Opossum. It's time to wake up."
"No," said Opossum. "It's time to sleep."

5.

6.

Center Connections ©1998 Monday Morning Books, Inc.

"Wake up, Robin. It's time to wake up."
"No," said Robin. "It's time to sleep."

7.

"Wake up, Bat. It's time to wake up."
"No," said Bat. "It's time to sleep."

3.

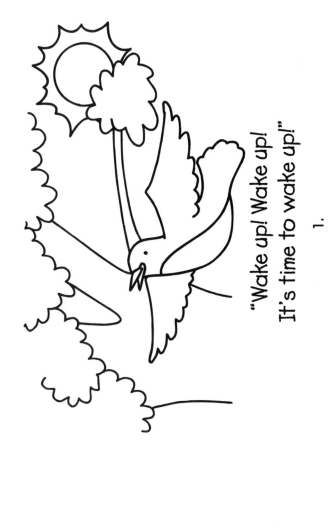

Wake Up! Wake Up!

"Wake up! Wake up!
It's time to wake up!"

1.

"Wake up, Owl. It's time to wake up."
"No," said Owl. "It's time to sleep."

2.

185

"Wake up, Opossum. It's time to wake up."
"No," said Opossum. "It's time to sleep."

5.

"Wake up, Robin. It's time to wake up."
"No," said Robin. "It's time to sleep."

7.

"Wake up, Raccoon. It's time to wake up."
"No," said Raccoon. "It's time to sleep."

4.

6.

SPRING

Take a walk with the children in early spring to look for signs of the new season. Make a list of all the things you noticed when you get back to the classroom.

Mural

Create a spring scene on a large piece of sky blue butcher paper. Glue light green hills from the skyline to the bottom of the paper after the children have fringed the curved edges. Have the children cut out colorful flowers to glue on the grass. Show them how to make fingerprint blossoms of pink and white on tree trunks and branches made with brown felt-tip markers.

Poetry Poster

Make a copy of the nursery rhyme "Humpty Dumpty" to put on a classroom bulletin board. Illustrate the poster with student-made Humpty Dumpties (on white drawing paper) sitting on red construction-paper walls with bricks marked off with black crayon.

Playhouse Transformations

For <u>March</u> ask the children to bring in empty cereal, frozen food, and cracker boxes to stock the shelves of the playhouse-turned-grocery store. Have the children make advertising signs for the walls and price tags for the shelves. Be sure to include a cash register (or tray) and plenty of "cash."

For <u>April</u>'s florist shop, collect silk and plastic flowers, various shaped plastic bottles to use as vases, and bows and ribbons to stick onto the arrangements. Have the children make signs and posters for the flower shop walls, and be sure to staple some blank papers together to serve as order pads. Again, the shop will need play money and a cash register.

Transform the playhouse into a business office for the month of <u>May</u>. Desks and chairs are important to an office and so are telephones. (You may be able to include a real telephone or two that no longer works.) Add an old typewriter that still works and lots of recycled paper, file folders, and file boxes. Put a can of pencils and pens and a calendar and blotter on each desk and watch the children go to work.

SEEDS AND PLANTS

Circle Time

Give each child a roasted peanut in the shell. Hand lenses would be useful too but are not necessary. Show the children how to take the shells off their peanuts and carefully break the peanuts in half with their thumb nails along the natural cracks. Almost every peanut has a tiny white plant in it which usually sticks to one of the two halves.

Tell the children that every seed has the beginning of a plant inside, even though it cannot always be seen. Talk about seeds and where they can be found. Ask if there are any other foods the children know of that have seeds in them. Before you begin these centers, have the children look for seeds at home to bring to school. Make some suggestions, such as seeds from apples, oranges, melons, and avocados; dried beans; and nuts. Send a note home telling parents about the project and asking them to help. Be sure to ask that the seeds be labeled.

As the children bring in their seeds and nuts to share, glue or tape samples of the different kinds to a large piece of poster board. Next to it write the name of the plant each seed will become. Look in seed catalogs for pictures to include.

Talk about the fact that nuts are seeds too. Explain that people do eat some nuts and seeds, but not all. Tell the children that some seeds are poisonous or are sprayed with chemicals, and should not be eaten. Remind them that they should never eat anything that comes from a plant without first asking a responsible grownup.

Explain the center activities.

 **Book List**

The Carrot Seed by Ruth Krauss (Harper and Row, 1945).
From Seed to Pear by Ali Mitgutsch (Carolrhoda Books, 1971).
Growing Vegetable Soup by Lois Elhert (Harcourt, Brace, Jovanovich, 1987).
Rabbit Seeds by Bijou Letord (Four Winds Press, 1984).
The Tiny Seed by Eric Carle (Picture Book Studio, 1987).

The Tiny Seed

Materials

Listening post and earphones
Tape recorder and blank cassette tape
At least one copy of the book
   The Tiny Seed by Eric Carle
Paper
Crayons
Flower seeds
Glue
Center poster

Teacher's Notes

• Tape record the story and gather the materials.
• Prepare and display the center poster.
• Demonstrate what the children do after they have heard the story.
  Make a sample picture to display in the center.

The Tiny Seed

1. Listen quietly to the story.

2. Make a picture story about a tiny seed:
   - Show the soil by coloring the lower part of your paper brown.
   - Glue a real seed in your soil.
   - Draw the roots, stem, leaves, and flowers with crayons.

Seed Mosaics

Materials

A variety of dry beans
Pieces of poster board (5 $\frac{1}{2}$" x 8 $\frac{1}{2}$"),
  1 for each child
White glue
Paper cups
Small paintbrushes

Teacher's Notes

• Gather the materials and prepare the student poster.
• Show the children how to sort each kind of bean into its own
  paper cup so that they can more easily arrange the colors and
  sizes the way that they like.
• Demonstrate each step of the activity. Place a sample in the
  center.

191

Seed Mosaics

1. Think about a design to make with the beans.

2. Use a brush to spread some glue on a small area of your cardboard.

3. Choose the beans you like. Set them close together in the glue in the design you decided on.

4. Spread some more glue onto another small part of your cardboard. Set more beans in place.

5. Continue covering your whole piece of cardboard in a colorful design.

Tasting 1, 2, 3

Materials

A variety of edible seeds and nuts
Nutcrackers (the bolt-action, twisting
   kind are best for children)
Paper towels
Large piece of poster board for graph
Center poster
Glue
Ruler

Teacher's Notes

- The following are nuts and edible seeds that are available at most local supermarkets: sunflower and pumpkin seeds, walnuts, almonds, pecans, pistachios, peanuts, and hazelnuts.

- Rule off the number of columns on the poster that correspond to the number of items the children will be tasting. Glue a different seed and/or nut at the top of each column.

- Make a sign for the graph that asks "Which seed do you like best?"
- Explain each step of the activity to the children. Be sure to show them how to use the nutcrackers.
- Be sure the children understand that nuts are seeds.
- Prepare and display the center poster.

Follow-up Activity

During a whole-group time after all the children have had a chance to do this center activity, discuss the graph together. Ask questions such as, "What does our graph show us about which seed we like the best?", "Which column is the longest?", "What does the longest column tell us?", etc.

Tasting 1, 2, 3

1. Taste one of each kind of seed.

2. Crack the nuts (which are also seeds) with the nutcracker. Taste one of each of them.

3. Glue the nut you like the best on the graph.

Bag Gardens

Materials

Resealable plastic sandwich bag for
   each child
Seeds (alfalfa or mung beans)
Masking tape and waterproof ink pen to
   label each child's bag
A needle
Bowls for warm water
Several trays on which to place the bags
   (cookie sheets work well)
Teaspoons

Teacher's Notes

- Gather the materials and prepare the student poster for display.
- Use the needle to make about 10 holes along the bottom of each
  plastic bag so that water can drain out of the bag.
- Demonstrate each step of the activity. Put a sample in the
  center.
- Show the children where to stick the name tape so that it will not
  disappear during the soaking phase.
- Provide a place that is not in the direct sun to put the trays
  of seeds.
- Remind the children to rinse and drain their seeds daily for
  four days.

1.

2.

3.

4.

5.

6.

Bag Gardens

1. Put your name on a piece of tape and stick it onto a plastic bag.

2. Put a teaspoon of seeds into the bag and zip it closed.

3. Place your bag in a small bowl of water to soak overnight.

4. The next day, drain your seeds well. Lay the bag on the tray near the window.

5. Rinse and drain the seeds every day for four days.

6. Put the sprouts in the sun on the fifth day.

7. How do the sprouts look different after a day in the sun?

8. Taste your sprouts. Take them home and make a sandwich to enjoy.

Seeds! Seeds!

Materials

Assembled student readers, 1 per child
Crayons
Sunflower seeds (or other large flat seeds)
White glue
Tagboard copies of the little Pointer Pal
  pattern, 1 per student
Strips of tagboard
Cellophane tape
Narrow-tip colored felt pens (for Pointer Pals)
Lengths of narrow ribbon, 1 per student
Scissors

Teacher's Notes for Student Readers

• Make copies of the student readers and assemble one per child.
  See the directions for assembling in the Introduction.
• Show the children which two pages to color each day.

Special Touch: When the children have finished coloring their
readers, give them each a large seed such as a sunflower seed to
glue onto the hand on page 1.

Notes for Pointer Pals

• When the student readers are complete, put the materials for
  making the Pointer Pals in the Reading Center. Show the children
  how to color and cut them out.
• Have an adult volunteer complete the students' Pointer Pals as
  described in the Introduction.

Pointer Pal Patterns ▭▶

Seeds! Seeds!

I planted some seeds.

1.

The seeds grew sprouts.

2.

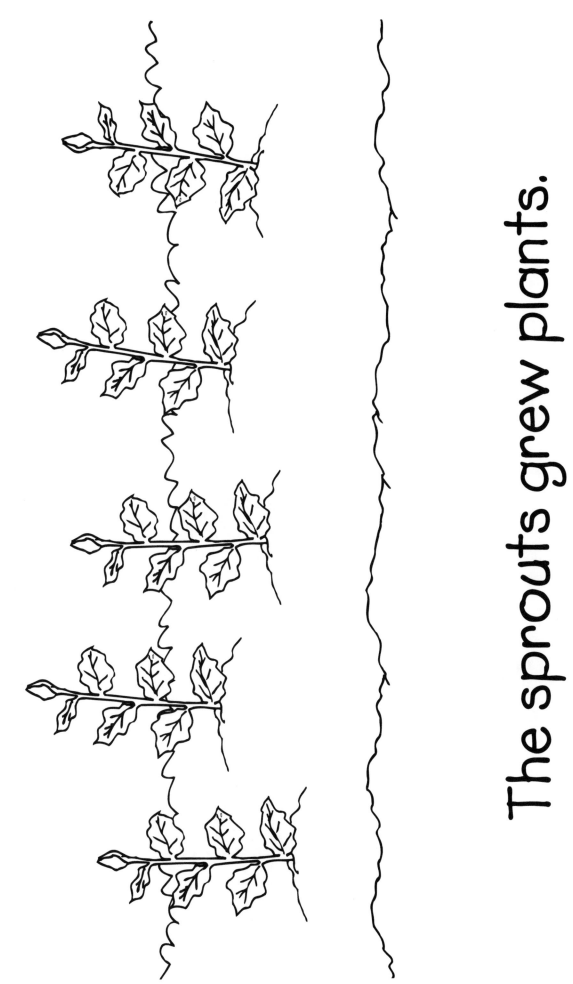

The sprouts grew plants.

3.

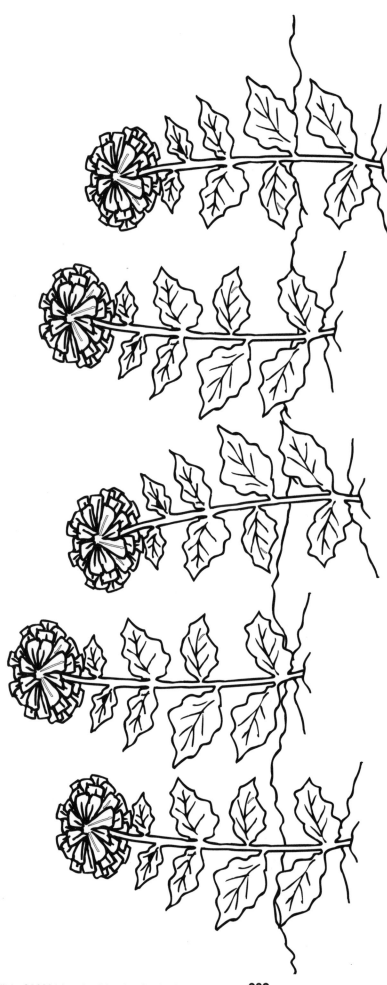

The plants grew flowers.

4.

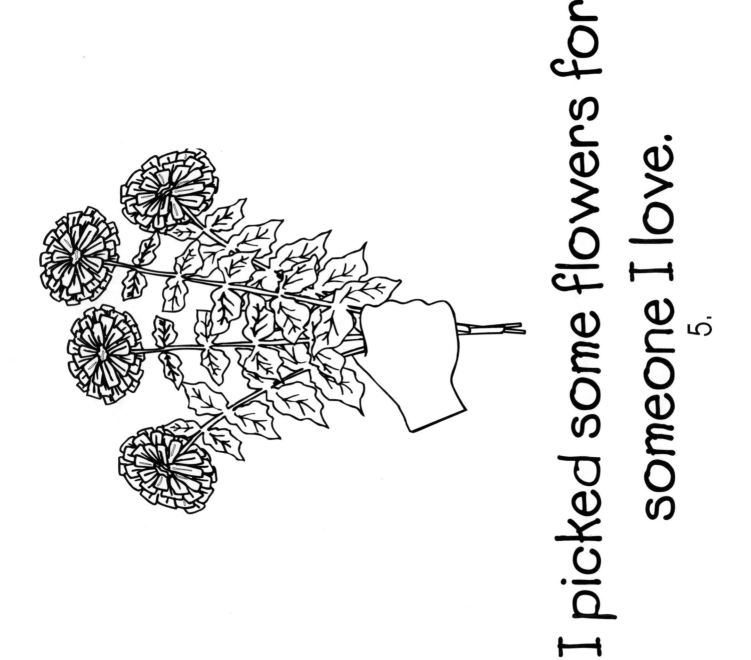

I picked some flowers for someone I love.

5.

The flowers grew seeds.

6.

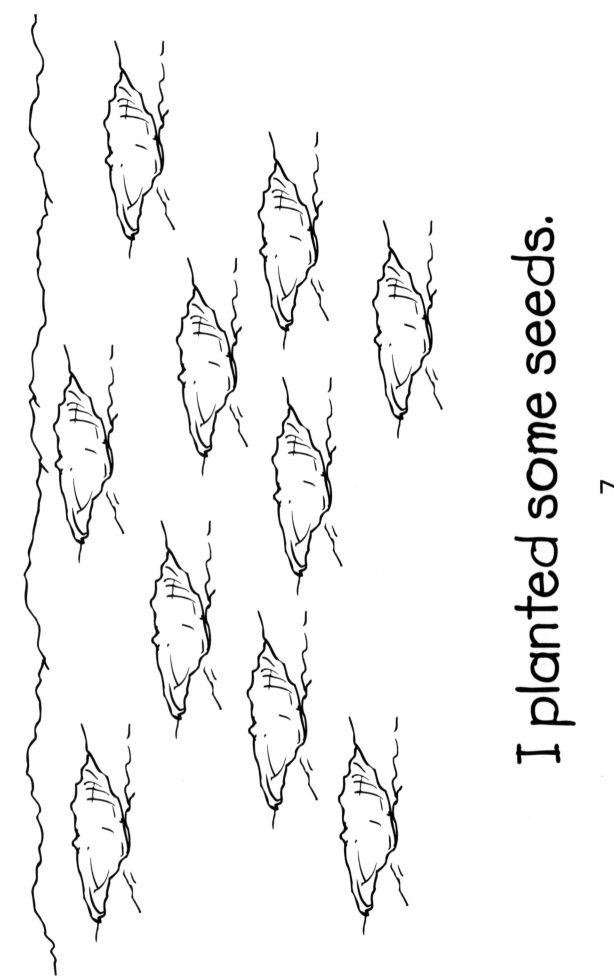

I planted some seeds.

7.

Seeds! Seeds!

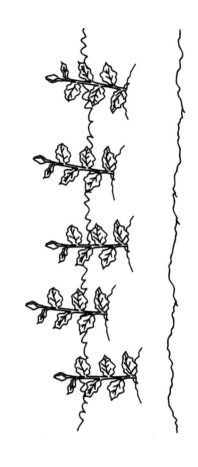

I planted some seeds.

1.

The sprouts grew plants.

3.

The seeds grew sprouts.

2.

I picked some flowers for someone I love.

5.

I planted some seeds.

7.

The plants grew flowers.

4.

The flowers grew seeds.

6.

EGGS

Circle Time

Different animals lay different types of eggs. Some animals lay large eggs and some lay small eggs. Some lay eggs with hard shells, some that are soft and rubbery, and some that are slippery. But whatever the kind of egg, the baby that hatches from it will grow up to look like its parents.

Make a poster of animals the children name. Draw a line down the center. On one side list the animals that hatch from eggs; on the other list those that are born live. Post the list and add to it as the children learn more about eggs in the following activities.

Explain the center activities.

 ## Book List

Chicken and Egg by Christine Back (Silver Burdette, 1984).

Chickens Aren't the Only Ones by Ruth Heller (Grossett and Dunlop, 1981).

The Chicken or the Egg? by Allan Fowler (Children's Press, 1993).

Eggs of Things by Maxine W. Kumin and Ann Sexton (G. P. Putnam's Sons, 1963).

An Extraordinary Egg by Leo Lionni (Alfred A. Knopf, 1994).

Rechenka's Eggs by Patricia Polacco (Philomel, 1988).

What's Inside by May Garelick (Scholastic Book Service, 1968).

Zinnia and Dot by Lisa Campbell Ernst (Viking, 1992).

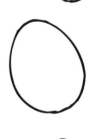

Chickens Aren't the Only Ones

Materials

A copy of the book *Chickens Aren't the Only Ones* by Ruth Heller
Earphones and listening post
Cassette recorder and blank tape
Crayons and pencils
Activity page

Teacher's Notes

- Gather the materials and prepare the center poster for display.
- Make one copy per child of the activity page.
- Tape the story.
- Explain the directions to the children.
- When all the children have completed the activity, collect their drawings and bind them together into a class book entitled "Our Egg Book."

Chickens Aren't the Only Ones

1. Listen quietly to the story.

2. When the story is finished, talk to another listener about the different animals that hatch from eggs.

3. Make a picture on the activity page of an animal that hatches from an egg.

4. Write the name of the animal on the line in the sentence.

_____ hatch from eggs too.

Chickens aren't the only ones.

_____ hatch from eggs too.

Chickens aren't the only ones.

Egg Prints

Materials

Plasticine clay
Construction paper (9" x 12")
Tempera paints
Paintbrushes

Teacher's Notes

- Gather the materials and prepare the center poster for display.
- Demonstrate the technique of molding the clay into an egg shape, then flattening it so the surface can be painted for print making.
- Model each step of the activity for the children. Put a sample in the center.

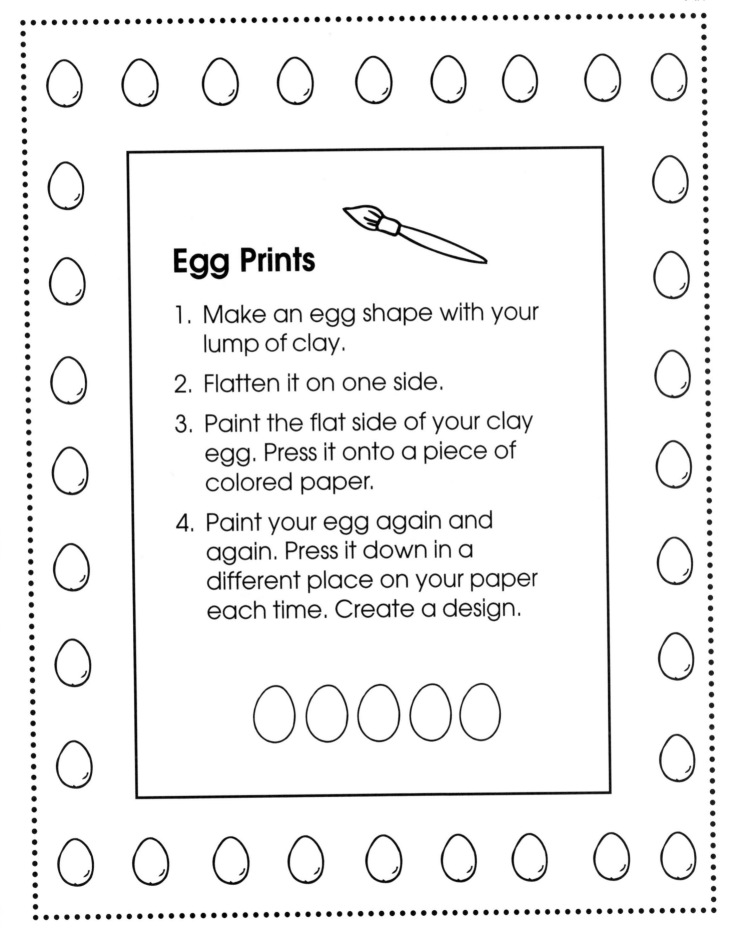

Egg Prints

1. Make an egg shape with your lump of clay.

2. Flatten it on one side.

3. Paint the flat side of your clay egg. Press it onto a piece of colored paper.

4. Paint your egg again and again. Press it down in a different place on your paper each time. Create a design.

Egg Patterns

Materials

"Egg Patterns" activity page
Construction paper
Scissors
Glue

Teacher's Notes

- Gather the materials and prepare the center poster for display.
- Make copies of the egg patterns page on various natural colors of construction paper (white, tan, and blue).
- Cut 4" x 18" strips of other colors of construction paper, one per child.
- Review the concept of linear patterning.
- Model each step of the activity for the children. Put a sample in the center.

Egg Patterns

1. Choose at least two different colored or different sized eggs.
2. Cut them out.
3. Arrange your egg shapes into a pattern you like.
4. Glue your pattern onto a strip of paper.

 Center Connections ©1998 Monday Morning Books, Inc.

Egg Patterns

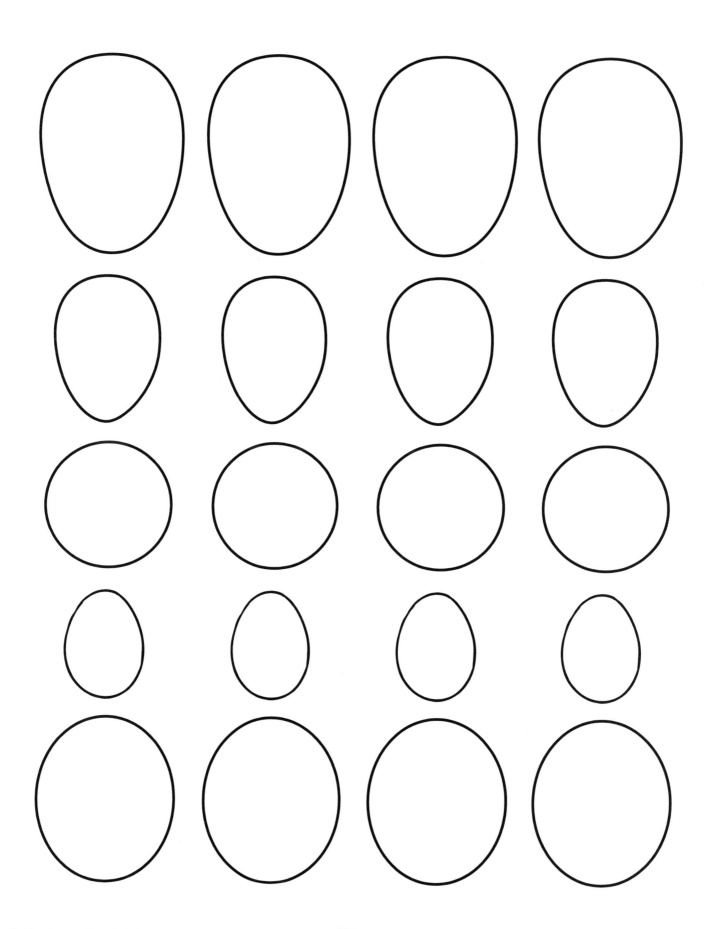

Egg-Zamination

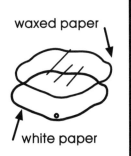

waxed paper

white paper

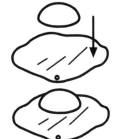

Materials

Raw chicken eggs, 1 per child
Dishes or paper plates, 1 per child
Hand lenses
Paper towels
Waxed paper
Copies of the Egg-Zamination activity page
Crayons
Scissors
Glue
Brads

brass fastener

Teacher's Notes

• Gather the materials and prepare the center poster for display.
• Make one copy of the activity page per student.
• Demonstrate step by step the cracking open of a raw egg. Show the children what to do about possible spills.
• Model all the steps of the activity. Make a sample to display in the center.

Egg-Zamination

1. Carefully break an egg into a dish.

2. Use a hand lens to look at the eggshell and the egg in the dish.

3. Talk with a friend about what you see. Name the parts of the egg together.

4. Make a model of the egg:
   - Color the egg yolk picture on the activity page. Make it the same color as the real egg. Cut it out.
   - Cut out the egg white pattern. Trace it onto waxed paper. Cut it out. Glue the waxed paper and the egg white pattern together.
   - Glue the egg yolk into the middle of the egg white.
   - Cut out the eggshell pieces pictured on the activity page.
   - Put the o's on the two eggshell pieces together. Push the points of a brad through both of them.
   - Push the brad through the o on the egg white and spread the points apart.

Egg-Zamination

Eggs
Science

Assembly of egg model:

waxed paper

white paper

brass fastener

219   *Center Connections* ©1998 Monday Morning Books, Inc.

An Egg

Materials

Assembled student readers
Crayons
Small yellow cotton balls
White glue
Strips of tagboard
Cellophane tape
Narrow-tip colored felt pens for Pointer Pals
Scissors
Lengths of narrow ribbon, 1 per student

Teacher's Notes for Student Readers

• See the directions for assembling the student readers in the Introduction. Make one reader per child.
• Show the children which two pages to color each day.

Special Touch: When the children have finished coloring all the pages in their student readers, give them each a yellow cotton ball to glue onto the body of the chick pictured on page 7.

Notes for Pointer Pals

• After the children have completed their readers, put the materials for making the Pointer Pals in the center. Show the children how to color and cut them out.
• Have an adult volunteer complete the students' Pointer Pals as described in the Introduction.

Pointer Pal Patterns ➡

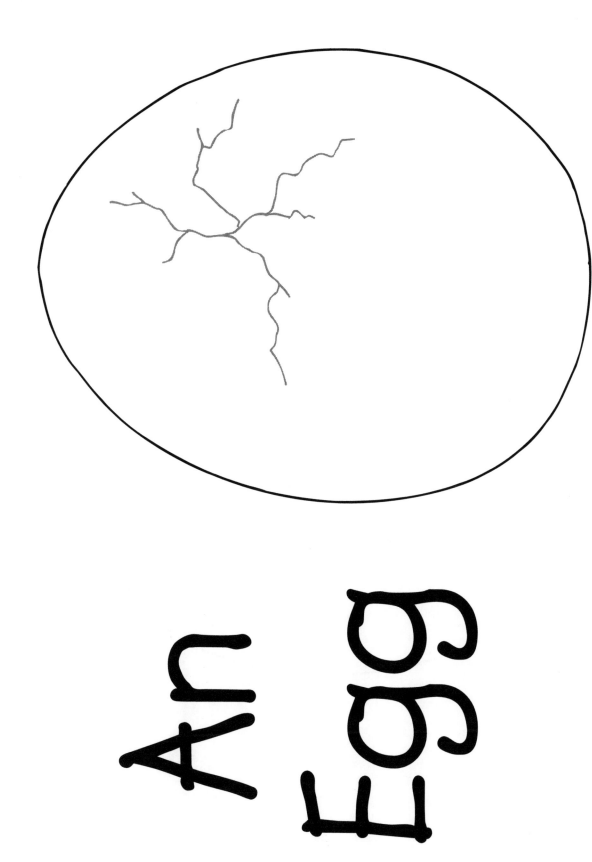

An Egg

Center Connections©1998 Monday Morning Books, Inc.

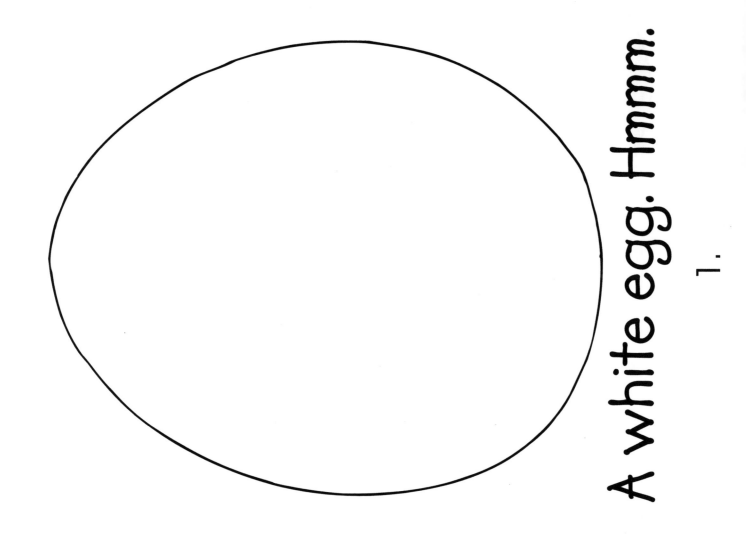

A white egg. Hmmm.

1.

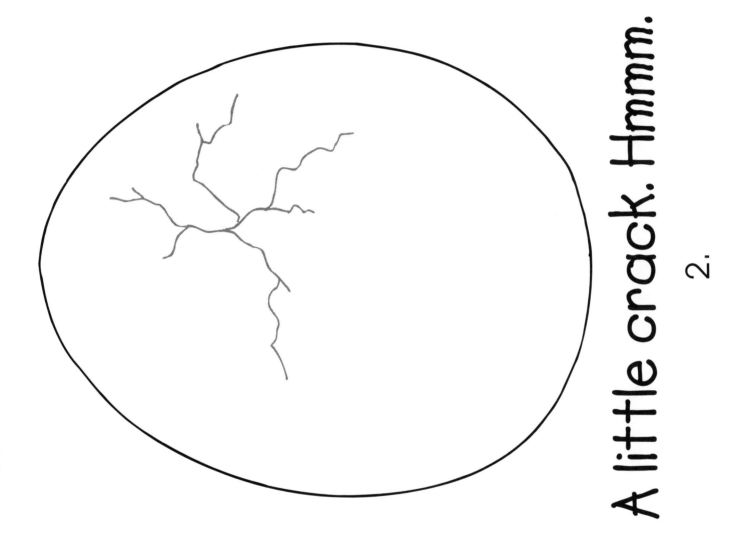

A little crack. Hmmm.

2.

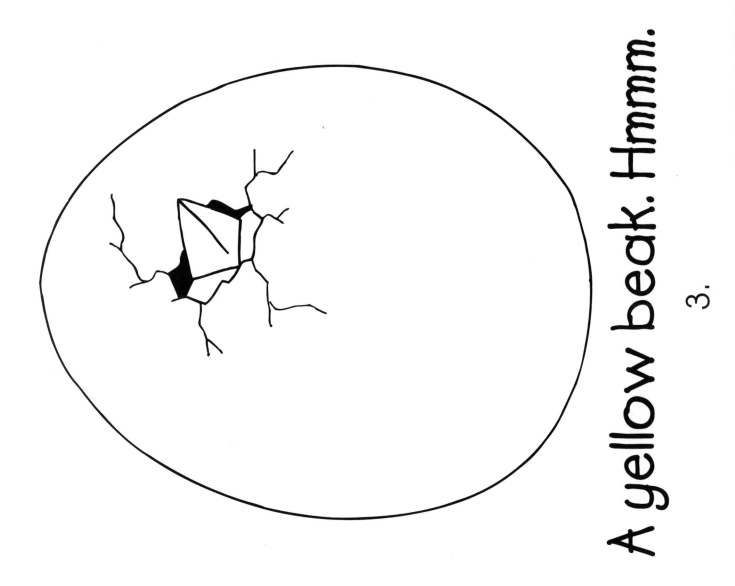

A yellow beak. Hmmm.

3.

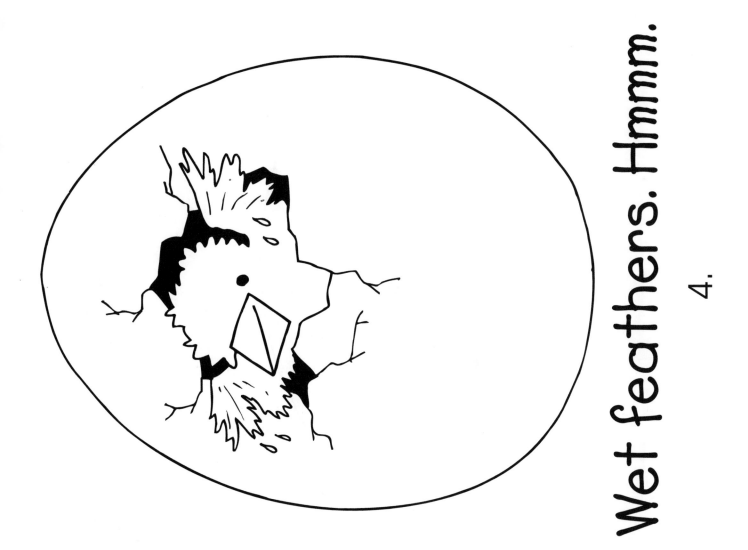

Wet feathers. Hmmm.

4.

Two little feet. Hmmm.

5.

A baby chick. Ahh.

6.

Peep! Peep! Peep!

7.

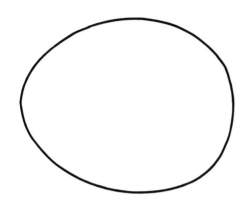

An Egg

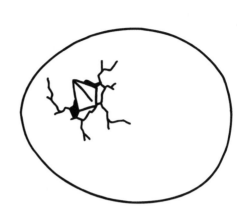

A white egg. Hmmm.

1.

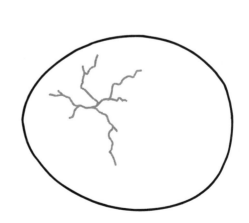

A yellow beak. Hmmm.

3.

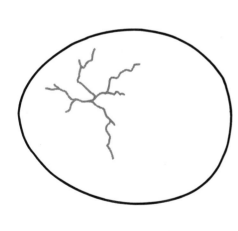

A little crack. Hmmm.

2.

Wet feathers. Hmmm.

4.

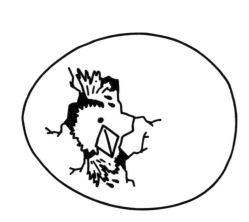

A baby chick. Ahh.

6.

Two little feet. Hmmm.

5.

Peep! Peep! Peep!

7.

BIRDS

Circle Time

Ask the children to think about birds and tell you something they know about them. Make a sentence list of their ideas on chart paper. (Examples: Birds have wings. They fly. Some birds swim. They have feathers and beaks. They lay eggs.)

Read the list and help the children compare the birds to other creatures with questions such as "Are birds the only creatures with wings?", "Name other animals with wings," "Can you think of any other animal that lays eggs?", "What other animals swim?"

After a short discussion, ask the children to think about something from the list that only birds have. Tell the children that feathers are what make a bird a bird.

Ask the children for the names of birds they know, and make a list to add to as the theme is developed.

Explain the center activities.

 **Book List**

Crinkleroot's Guide to Knowing the Birds by Jim Arnosky (Macmillan, 1992).
Feathers for Lunch by Lois Elhert (Voyager Books, 1990).
Good Night, Owl by Pat Hutchins (Macmillan, 1972).
Have You Seen Birds? by Joanne Oppenheim (Scholastic, 1986).
Make Way for Ducklings by Robert McCloskey (Viking, 1941).
Round Robin by Jack Kent (Prentice-Hall, 1982).
What Makes a Bird a Bird by May Garelick (Follett Publishing Co., 1969).
Who Took the Farmer's Hat? by Joan Nodset (Harper Collins, 1963).

Good Night, Owl

Materials

At least one copy of the book *Good Night, Owl* by Pat Hutchins
Listening post and earphones
Cassette recorder and blank cassette tape
Drawing paper and crayons

Teacher's Notes

• Tape the story and gather the materials.
• Prepare the center poster for display.
• Review the directions on the center poster.
• After all of the children have completed the listening activity, bind their pictures together into a class book entitled "Good Night, Birds." Put the book in the classroom library.

Good night, penguin.

Good night, cardinal.

Good night sparrow.

Good night, ostrich.

Good night, hummingbird.

Good Night, Owl

1. Listen quietly to the story.

2. When the story is finished, talk to the listener next to you about your favorite bird.

3. Color a picture of your favorite bird.

4. Write a sentence under your picture that contains the name of your favorite bird.

   Good night, _____.

   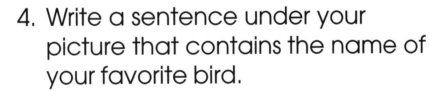

(Write the name of your favorite bird in the space where the line is.)

Bottle Birds

Materials

Magazines
Scissors
Glue or paste
Colored pens
Construction paper (9" x 12") in a variety
of colors

Teacher's Notes

• Cut some pictures of bottles from magazines to use as examples in your explanation of what the children will be doing.
• Introduce the activity by showing the children some pictures of birds. Point out the wings, beak, tail feathers, etc. Then demonstrate each step of the activity.
• Prepare the center poster for display. Gather and lay out the materials.

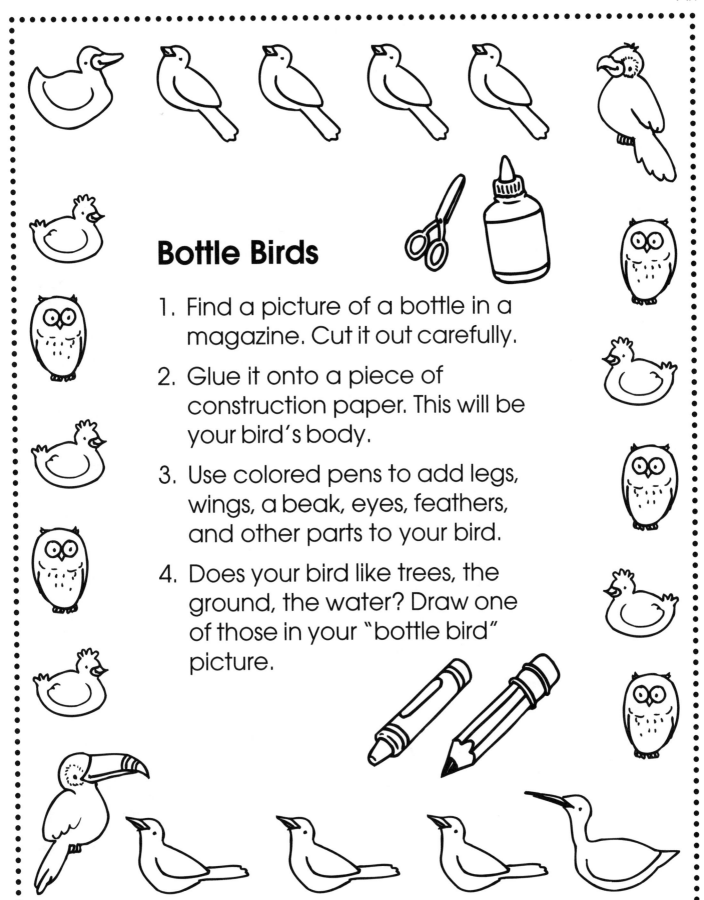

Bottle Birds

1. Find a picture of a bottle in a magazine. Cut it out carefully.

2. Glue it onto a piece of construction paper. This will be your bird's body.

3. Use colored pens to add legs, wings, a beak, eyes, feathers, and other parts to your bird.

4. Does your bird like trees, the ground, the water? Draw one of those in your "bottle bird" picture.

Bird Watchers

Materials

Empty toilet paper tubes, 2 per child
Yarn
Copies of "Bird Watcher's Tally"
Clipboards or sturdy pieces of cardboard
   with clothespin "clip," 1 per child
Stapler and staples
Scissors

Teacher's Notes

- Gather the materials and prepare the center poster for display.
- Prepare binoculars by stapling two toilet paper tubes together for each child. Attach a two-foot length of yarn to the top of each set to serve as a neck strap.
- Explain that using tally marks is a quick way to record how many of something you have. The children will be making a tally mark each time they see a bird in a particular place, such as a tree, on the grass, or on the power lines or a fence. Help the children to understand that they must mark where they first see a bird; for example, if a bird is in a tree and flies to the grass while the child is watching, the tally must be marked in the "tree" column of the "Bird Watcher's Tally."
- Demonstrate each step of the activity for the children.

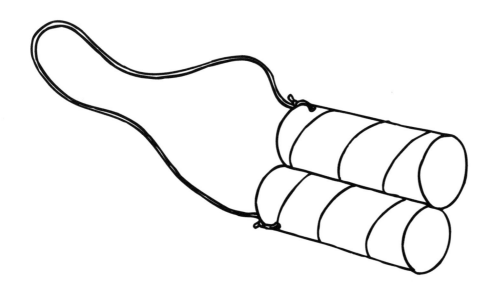

Bird Watchers

1. Go outside with a clipboard, "Bird Watcher's Tally" sheet, pencil, and binoculars. Look for birds.

2. For every bird you see, make a tally mark on your sheet. Put the mark in the place that tells where you first saw the bird.

3. Count the number of birds you saw. Where were the most birds?

4. When you have counted at least five birds, talk about your tally sheet with a bird-watching friend.

Bird Watcher's Tally

Birds I saw in a tree or bush

Birds I saw on the ground

Birds I saw flying

Birds I saw on a wire or fence

Our Feathered Friends

Materials

Natural feathers (available at craft and
    school-supply stores)
Hand lenses
Drawing paper
Pencils
Crayons
Small containers of water
Paper towels
Eyedroppers
String
Scissors
Transparent tape

Teacher's Notes

- Gather and lay out the materials. Prepare the center poster
  for display.
- Demonstrate the use of the hand lenses and eyedroppers as you
  model each step of the activity. Explain that these are tools scientists use to learn about things, and that in this activity they will be
  scientists learning about feathers.
- Model each step of the activity.

Our Feathered Friends

1. Choose a feather to learn about.

2. Measure your feather by cutting a piece of string that is the same length. Tape the string on a piece of drawing paper.

3. Look at your feather with a hand lens. Talk to someone about what you see.

4. Draw your feather. Use the colors you see on your feather.

5. Put a drop of water on your feather. Talk to a friend about what happens.

6. On your activity sheet, draw a picture of the bird you think your feather came from.

7. Write your name on your paper.

Birds

Materials

Assembled student readers, 1 per child
Crayons
Small feathers (packages of feathers are
    available at craft stores)
White glue
Strips of tagboard
Cellophane tape
Narrow-tip colored felt pens for Pointer Pals
Scissors
Lengths of narrow ribbon, 1 per child

Teacher's Notes for Student Readers

• See the directions for assembling the student readers in the
  Introduction. Make one reader per child.
• Show the children which two pages to color each day.

Special Touch: When the children have finished coloring the
pages of their readers, give each of them some small feathers to glue
on to page 2.

Notes for Pointer Pals

• After the children have completed their readers, put the materials
  for making the Pointer Pals in the Reading Center. Show the
  children how to color and cut them out.
• Have an adult volunteer complete the students' Pointer Pals as
  described in the Introduction.

Pointer Pal Patterns ⟿➡

Center Connections ©1998 Monday Morning Books, Inc.

Birds

We are birds.

1.

We have feathers.

2.

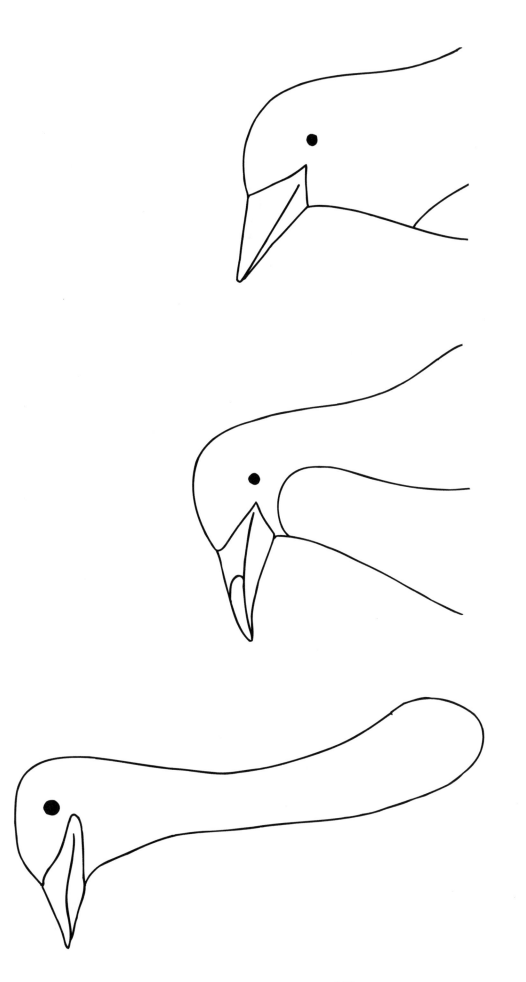

We have beaks.

3.

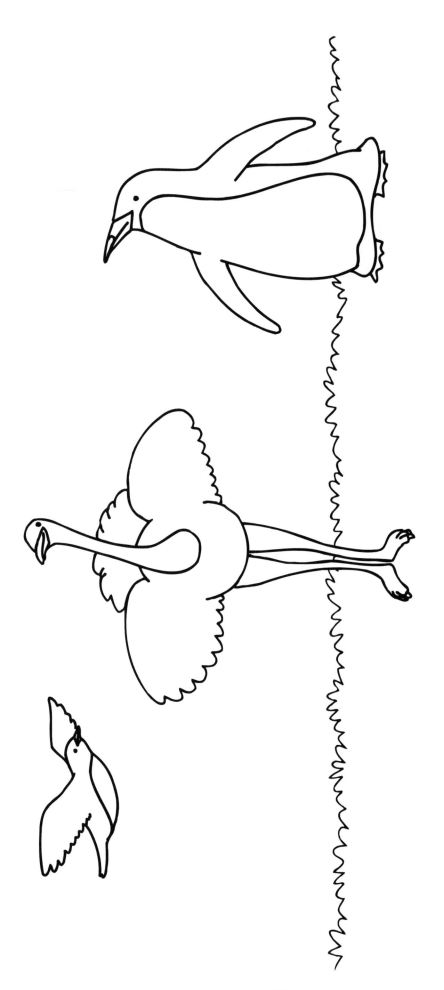

We have wings.

4.

"I can fly," said the robin.

5.

"I can't fly, but I can run,"
said the ostrich.

6.

"I can't fly, but I can swim," said the penguin.

7.

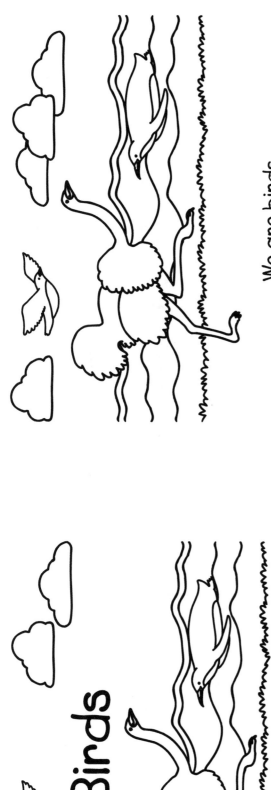

Birds

We are birds.

1.

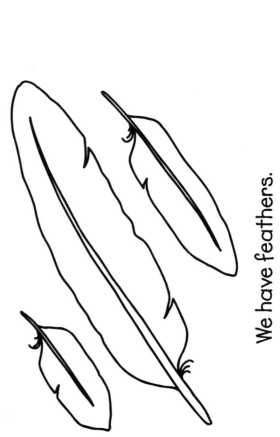

We have feathers.

2.

We have beaks.

3.

"I can fly," said the robin.

5.

"I can't fly, but I can swim," said the penguin.

7.

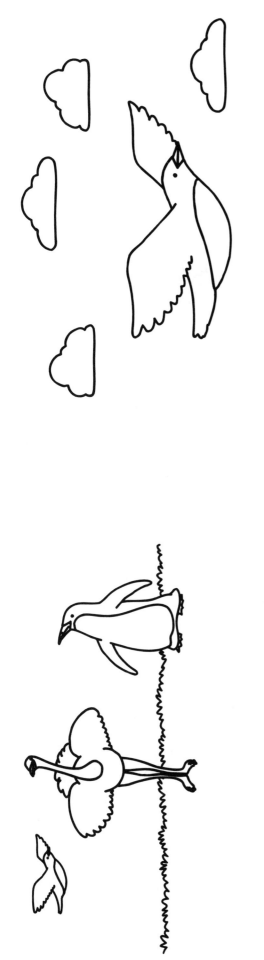

We have wings.

4.

"I can't fly, but I can run," said the ostrich.

6.

WIND

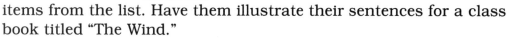

Circle Time

Read one of the books about wind listed below. Discuss and make a list of the things that the children have seen the wind blow (a person's hair, an umbrella, the sand, etc.). Have the children complete a sentence, such as, "The wind blew_____," with one of the items from the list. Have them illustrate their sentences for a class book titled "The Wind."

Explain the center activities.

 ## Book List

Catch the Wind by Gail Gibbons (Little, Brown, 1989).
Gilberto and the Wind by Marie Hal Ets (Puffin Books, 1978).
The Girl Who Loved the Wind by Jane Yolen
    (Harper and Row, 1987).
Millicent and the Wind by Robert Munsch
    (Firefly Books, 1988).
Peter and the North Wind retold by Freya Littledale
    (Scholastic Inc., 1988).
When the Wind Stops by Charlotte Zolotow
    (Harper Collins, 1990).
The Wind Blew by Pat Hutchins (Puffin, 1974).

Peter and the North Wind

Materials

At least one copy of the book *Peter and the North Wind* retold by Freya Littledale
Listening post and earphones
Tape recorder and blank cassette tape
Crayons
Drawing paper

Teacher's Notes

• Tape the story and gather the materials.
• Duplicate copies of the activity page, one per child.
• Prepare and display the center poster.
• Tell the children to listen carefully to the story so that they can draw the three things that the North Wind gives to the little boy named Peter.

Peter and the North Wind

1. Listen quietly to the story.

2. Talk to the listener next to you about the three things the North Wind gave to Peter.

3. Draw three big clouds in a row on your paper. Number them using very small numbers. Draw the first thing the North Wind gave to Peter in cloud number 1. Draw the second thing in cloud number 2. Draw the third in cloud number 3.

Windsocks

Materials

Light, flexible cardboard or heavy paper in
  a variety of colors
Colored tissue or crepe paper in a variety
  of colors
Colored felt-tip markers
White glue
Stapler and staples
String
Scissors

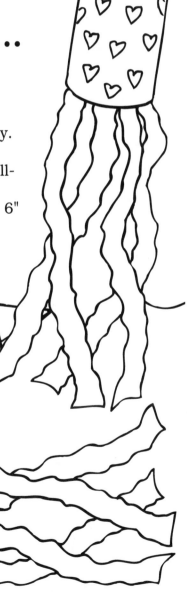

Teacher's Notes

- Cut the heavy paper or cardboard into strips about 6" wide by
  18" long.
- Gather all the materials and prepare the center poster for display.
- Model the directions, discussing each step as you go.
- Give suggestions for decorating the piece of cardboard with an all-
  over design of colorful stripes, zigzags, stars, etc.
- Help the children form the tagboard into a cylinder, stapling the 6"
  ends together. Display a sample in the center.

Windsocks

1. Make a colorful design all over the cardboard.

2. Bend the cardboard into a ring. Staple the short sides together.

3. Glue paper streamers along the bottom of the cardboard ring.

4. Staple three strings to the top of the cardboard ring. Tie their ends together.

5. Tie a longer piece of string to the knotted end. Use this piece to hang your windsock from the branch of a tree.

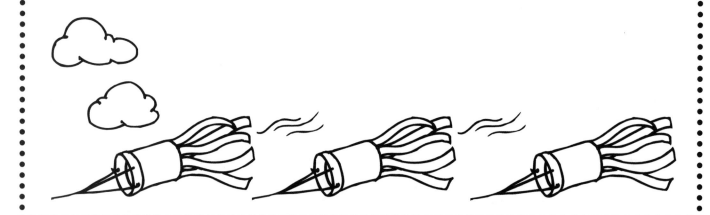

Blow by Blow

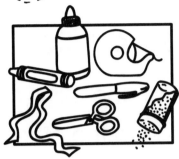

Materials

Drinking straws, 1 per child
Container filled with a variety of objects
(cotton balls, marbles, leaves, crayons,
large paper clips, wads of newspaper about
2" in diameter)
Recording graph activity page
Pencils
Masking tape

Teacher's Notes

- Make a copy of the recording graph activity page for each child.
- Gather materials and prepare and display the center poster.
- Demonstrate blowing through a straw so that a stream of air is directed toward an object to be moved.
- Model each step of the activity for the children.
- Place a piece of masking tape on a table for the starting line. Place another about three feet away for the finish line.

Blow by Blow

1. Put one thing on the starting line.

2. Move the object by blowing at it through a straw. Count how many blows it takes to get the object to the finish line.

3. Record on your graph how many blows it took to get the object to the finish line.

4. Put another object on the starting line. Blow it across the finish line. Record on the graph how many blows it took.

5. Do the same with each of the objects.

6. Talk to a friend about these questions:
   • Which object was the hardest to move?
   • Which object was the easiest to move?

Blow by Blow

Name _____

Blow by Blow

	1	2	3	4	5	6	7	8	9	10	11	12	13	14
cotton ball														
marble														
leaf														
crayon														
paper clip														
paper														

Pinwheel Hats

Materials

Pinwheel pattern
Flexible cardboard for headbands
Pine or balsa-wood lath ($^3/_4$" by $^1/_2$")
Masking tape
Straight pins
Small plastic beads
Small hammer
Colored felt pens
Scissors
Stapler and staples
Copy paper

Teacher's Notes

- Make a copy of the pinwheel pattern on regular copy paper for each child.
- Cut the lath into 4" lengths.
- Gather the materials and prepare and display the center poster.
- Adult assistants will be needed to assemble the pinwheels and attach them to the lath and the headband. The children will also need someone to adjust the headband size to each of their heads.
- Model the steps for construction for both the assistants and the students. (See the construction directions on the pinwheel pattern.) Display the pinwheel hat in the center.

Pinwheel Hats

1. Decorate your headband strip and the pinwheel pattern with felt markers.

2. Ask a grown-up to staple the headband in a circle that fits around your head.

3. Carefully cut the pinwheel pattern along the black lines.

4. Have a grown-up help you assemble the pinwheel and tape it to your headband.

5. Go outside and let the wind make your pinwheel spin.

6. Find out the answers to these questions:
   - Will the pinwheel spin when you stand still?
   - Can you make it stop?
   - What can you do to make it spin fast?

Pinwheel Pattern

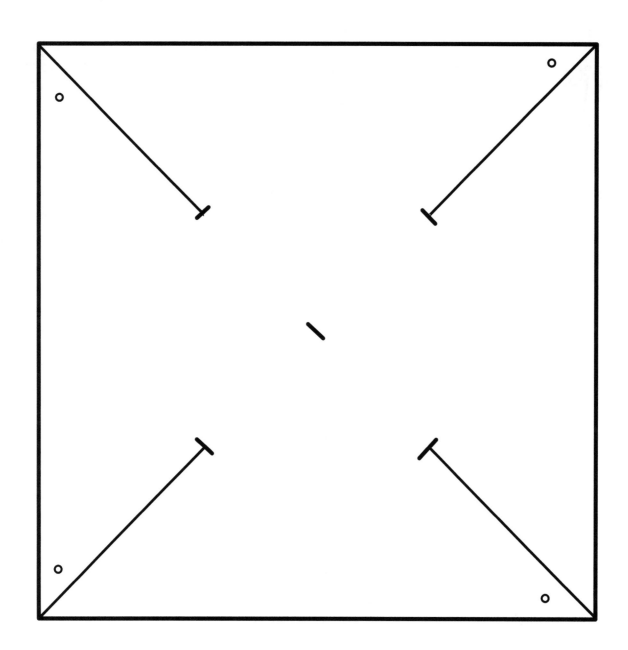

Cut.

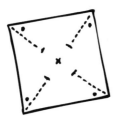

Assemble.

Attach.

Blow, Wind, Blow

Materials

Assembled student readers, 1 per child
Crayons
White absorbent cotton
White glue
Tagboard copies of the little Pointer Pal
    pattern, 1 per student
Strips of tagboard
Cellophane tape
Narrow-tip colored felt pens (for Pointer Pals)
Lengths of narrow ribbon, 1 per student
Scissors

Teacher's Notes for Student Readers

- Make copies of the student readers and assemble one per child. See the directions for assembling in the Introduction.
- Show the children which two pages to color each day.

Special Touch: When the children have finished coloring their readers, have them glue a thin layer of absorbent cotton onto the picture of the clouds on the center of the book

Notes for the Pointer Pals

- When the student readers are complete, put the materials for making the Pointer Pals in the center. Show the children how to color and cut them out.
- Have an adult volunteer complete the students' Pointer Pals as described in the Introduction.

Pointer Pal Patterns ⅢⅢ➡

Blow, Wind, Blow!

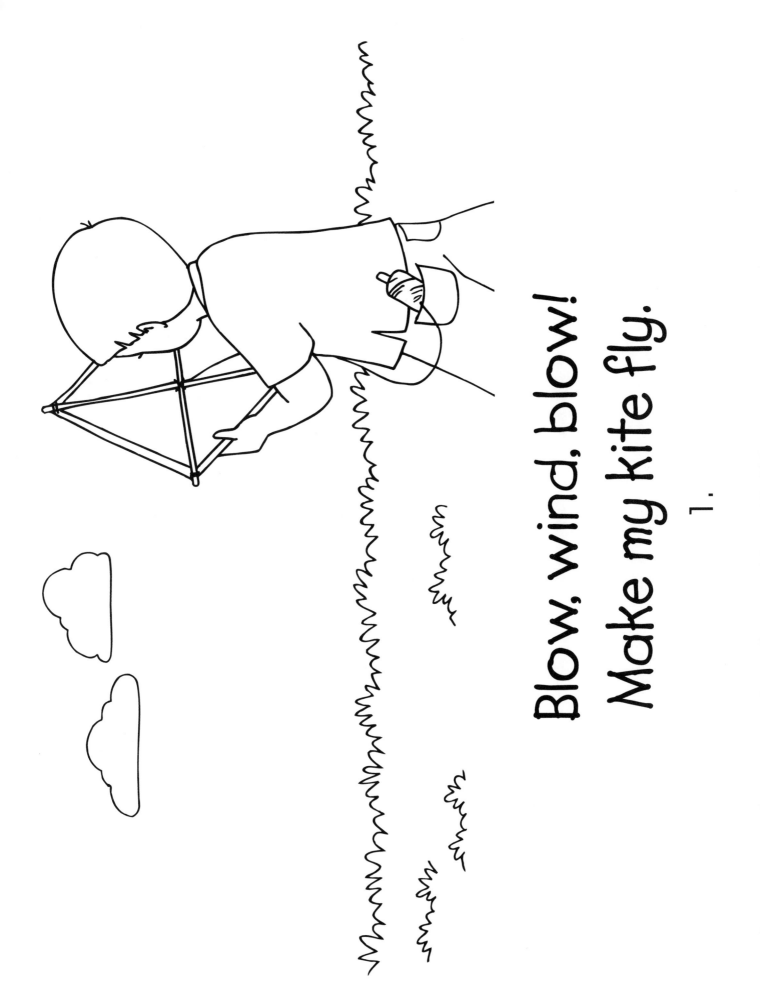

Blow, wind, blow!
Make my kite fly.

1.

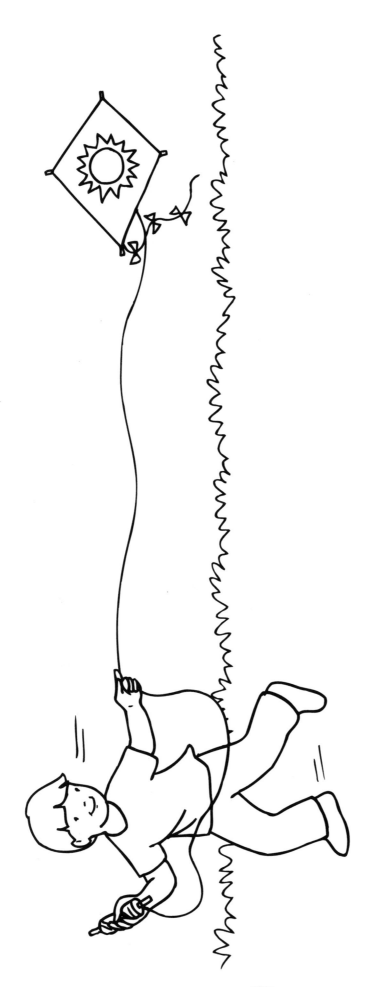

Blow, wind, blow!
Make my kite fly high.
2.

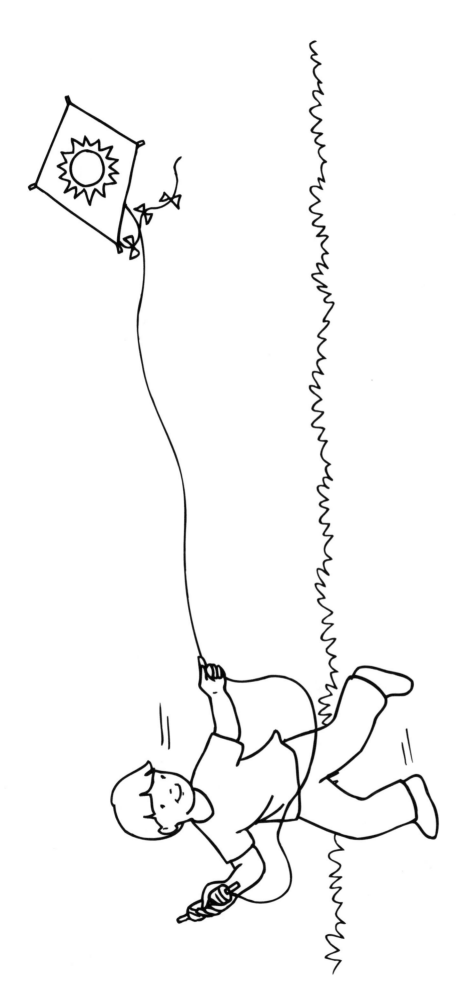

Blow, wind, blow!
Make my kite fly very high.

3.

Center Connections ©1998 Monday Morning Books, Inc.

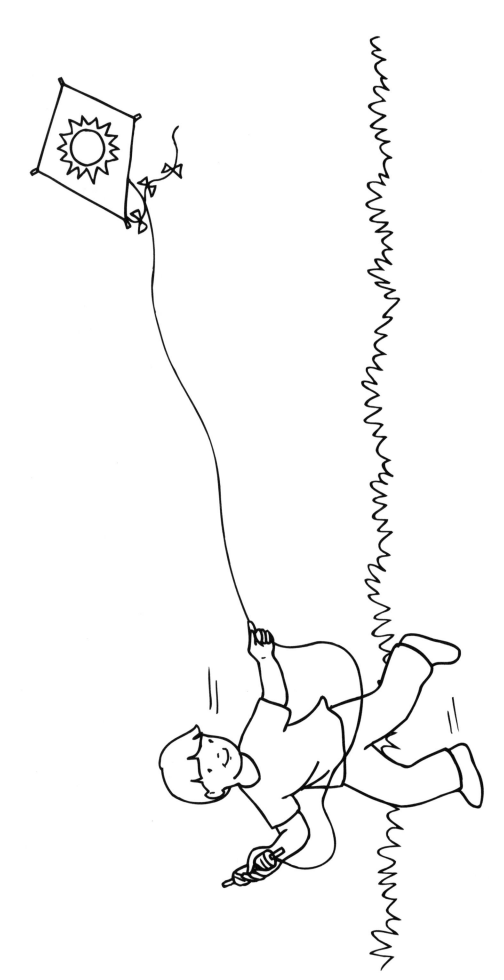

Blow, wind, blow!
Make my kite fly high above the earth.

4.

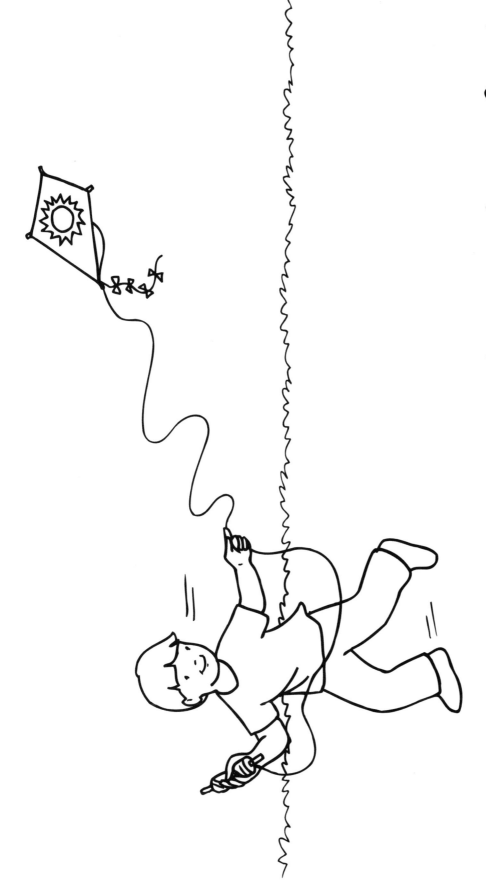

Blow, wind, blow! Make my kite fly high above the earth and the clouds.

5.

Oops!

6.

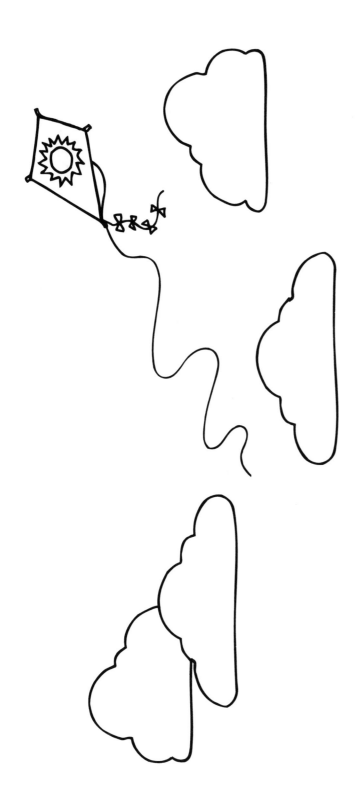

Stop, wind, stop!
Make my kite come down.

7.

Blow, Wind, Blow!

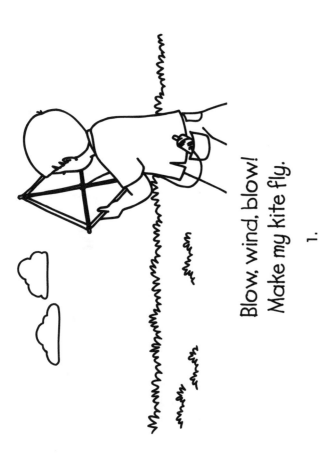

Blow, wind, blow!
Make my kite fly.

1.

Blow, wind, blow!
Make my kite fly high.

2.

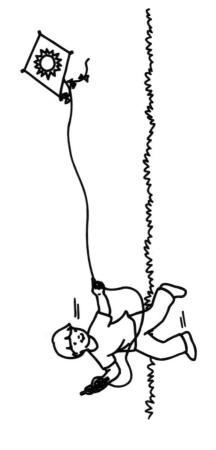

Blow, wind, blow!
Make my kite fly very high.

3.

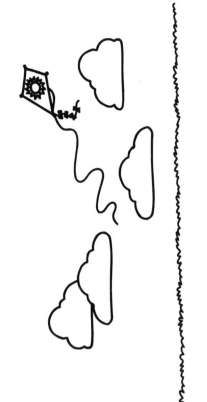

Stop, wind, stop!
Make my kite come down.

7.

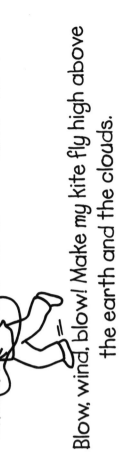

Blow, wind, blow! Make my kite fly high above
the earth and the clouds.

5.

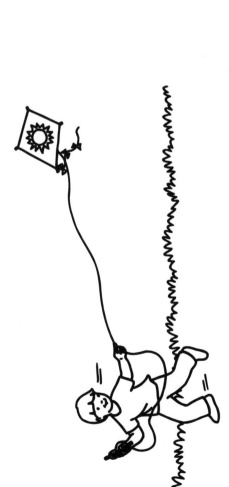

Blow, wind, blow!
Make my kite fly high above the earth.

4.

Oops!

6.

SUMMER

Talk with the children about what the summer season is like. Ask them what they like to do in the summer. Make a summer fun list. Have the children draw a picture of themselves in the summer doing their favorite activity. Display their drawings around the summer fun list.

Mural

Make an "under the sea" mural. Start with blue background paper and cut out and glue on lots of sea life created by the children with felt pens and drawing paper. Be sure to include seaweed and coral. Have some of the children try out their artistic talents designing a shipwreck for the ocean floor.

Poetry Poster

Make a copy of the nursery rhyme "Mary, Mary, Quite Contrary" on a piece of poster board. Give the children an assortment of various kinds and colors of paper (tissue, wrapping, crepe, etc.) and have each create a unique flower for Mary's garden. Post the poem and decorate the wall around it with the special flowers.

Playhouse Transformation

Change the playhouse into a fast-food restaurant for June. Let the children decide what kinds of food they will be selling and have them make signs indicating how much each item will cost. Hamburgers, milkshakes, and fries are popular choices. Provide play money and a cash register, if possible, or a cash drawer. The "servers" can wear hats made from four-inch strips of white construction paper stapled to fit around their heads. The "customers" may want to make a wallet or coin purse from brown or black construction paper glued or stapled into a pocket or envelope shape.

ROCKS

Circle Time

Ask the children if they have ever found a rock that they have wanted to keep. Discuss what the rock looked like, where they found it, and why they liked it so much. Show them a rock that you like and tell them why you like it. Ask them to bring their favorite rock to school to put on display.

Read *Everybody Needs a Rock* by Byrd Baylor (Macmillan, 1974). Tell the children that they will be collecting, observing, sorting, and studying rocks just like the scientists called geologists do.

Explain the center activities.

📚 Book List

Anansi and the Moss-Covered Rock retold by Eric A. Kimmel (Scholastic, 1988).

Everybody Needs a Rock by Byrd Baylor (Macmillan, 1974).

It Could Still Be a Rock by Allan Fowler (Children's Press, 1993).

On My Beach There Are Many Pebbles by Leo Lionni (Astor-Honor, 1961).

Sylvester and the Magic Pebble by William Steig (Simon and Schuster, 1969).

276

Sylvester and the Magic Pebble

Materials

A copy of the book *Sylvester and the Magic Pebble* by William Steig
Listening post and earphones
Tape recorder and blank cassette tape
Drawing paper and crayons

Teacher's Notes

• Tape the story. Gather the materials.
• Explain to the children that in the story Sylvester makes a wish that comes true and causes him lots of trouble. Tell them that after they have listened to the story they should use their imaginations and draw a picture to show what they might wish for if they found a magic pebble.
• Prepare and display the center poster.

Sylvester and the Magic Pebble

1. Listen quietly to the story.
2. Talk to the listener sitting next to you about a wish you would like to come true.
3. Draw a picture about your wish. Write or tell a story.
4. Put your name on your picture.

Rock Art

Materials

A variety of small rocks and pebbles
Corrugated cardboard
White glue and wheat paste
Craft sticks, 1 per child
Small paper cups
Scissors

Teacher's Notes

- Cut the corrugated cardboard into 4" x 6" pieces.
- Prepare the glue mixture just before use by stirring white glue into one cup of wheat paste until it's the consistency of mashed potatoes.
- Put the mixture into paper cups, one per child.
- Gather the materials and prepare and display the center poster.
- Model the steps of this activity for the children. Be sure to demonstrate the use of a craft stick rather than hands to apply the glue mixture to the sculpture. Make a sample to display in the center.

279

Rock Art

1. As you do this activity, be sure to use a stick to put the blobs of glue on your creation.
2. Glue a rock that you like onto your cardboard.
3. Choose other rocks to glue onto your work of art one at a time. Hold each one in place for a few seconds for the glue to set.
4. Make your artwork taller by gluing rocks on top of each other.

Pebble Grab

Materials

Drawing paper
Small pails or paper cups of pebbles
Pencils
Activity page

Teacher's Notes

- Pebbles are available at rockeries and pet or aquarium supply stores. They should be between $1/4$" and $1/2$" in diameter.
- Make copies of the activity page, one per student.
- Explain to the children that an estimate is like a guess. Encourage them to make estimates without being too concerned about correctness. Tell them that estimating is a technique scientists use in their work.
- Prepare and display the center poster.
- Demonstrate each step of the activity for the children.

Pebble Grab

1. Put your name on a piece of drawing paper.

2. Trace your hands. Put an R under the drawing of your right hand. Put an L under the drawing of your left hand.

3. Estimate how many pebbles you can grab in your right hand. Write the number you estimate on the drawing of your right hand.

4. Use your right hand. Take a handful of pebbles. Count the pebbles and write the number on the drawing of your right hand. Put a circle around that number.

5. Estimate how many pebbles you can grab in your left hand. Write the number you estimate on the drawing of your left hand.

6. Use your left hand. Take a handful of pebbles. Count the pebbles and write the number on the drawing of your left hand. Put a circle around that number.

7. Look at the circled numbers on your drawings. Are they the same? Is one a lot more than the other or just a little bit more?

Rock Hounds

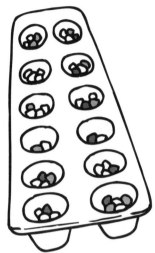

Materials

Paper lunch bags, 1 per child
Hand lenses
Tub of water
Egg cartons, 1 per child
Digging tools
Paper towels

Teacher's Notes

- Take the children on a rock-hunting expedition. Rocks can be found almost everywhere; even if the children can only go right outside the classroom they are bound to make some interesting finds. (To ensure this, however, you may wish to help nature along by gathering rocks ahead of time from another area and scattering them where the children will be looking.)

- Before going out, show the children an egg carton. Tell them that each of them will have one to use as a collection box. Count the sections and explain they are to bring in just that many rocks, and that each rock must fit in a section. (This limits the size and quantity of the rocks.)

- Define the area where the children may search for their rocks. Prepare a tub of water for washing them where spillage will not be a problem.

- Encourage the children to look for many different kinds of rocks for their collections.

- Gather the materials and prepare and display the center poster.

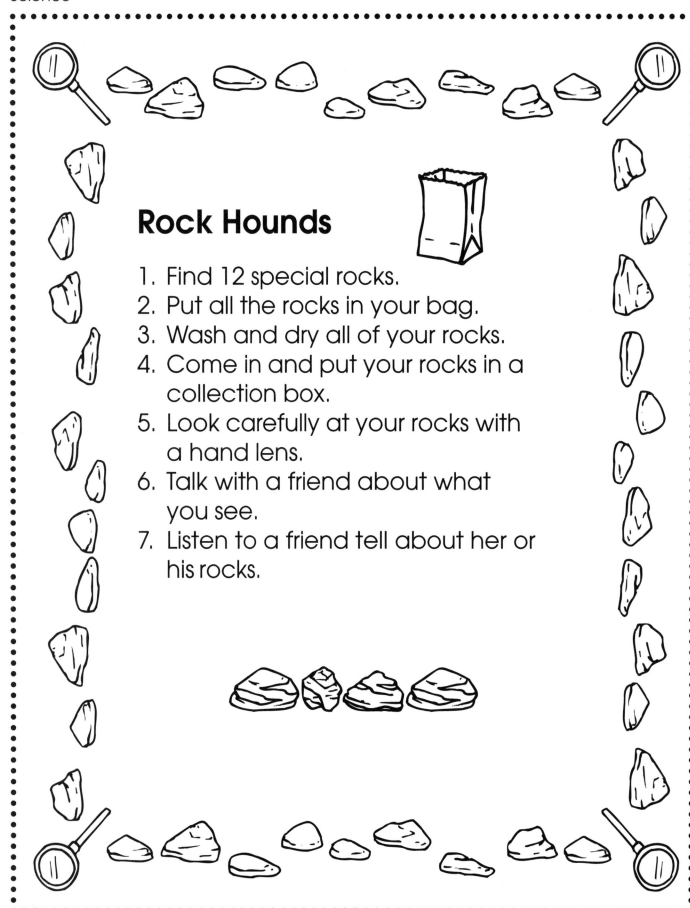

Rock Hounds

1. Find 12 special rocks.
2. Put all the rocks in your bag.
3. Wash and dry all of your rocks.
4. Come in and put your rocks in a collection box.
5. Look carefully at your rocks with a hand lens.
6. Talk with a friend about what you see.
7. Listen to a friend tell about her or his rocks.

All Kinds of Rocks

Materials

Assembled student readers, 1 per child (see
  "Teacher's Notes for Student Readers,"
  below)
White construction paper
Crayons
Small pebbles (available at aquarium-
  supply stores)
White glue
Tagboard copies of the little Pointer Pal pattern, 1 per student
Strips of tagboard
Cellophane tape
Narrow-tip colored felt pens for Pointer Pals
Lengths of narrow ribbon, 1 per student
Scissors

Teacher's Notes for Student Readers

• Make the copies of these student readers on white construction
  paper following the directions for assembling them in the
  Introduction.
• Show the children which two pages to color each day.

Special Touch: When the children have finished coloring their
readers, give each of them two or three very small pebbles to glue
onto the cover.

Notes for Pointer Pals

• When the student readers are complete, put the materials for
  making the Pointer Pals in the center. Show the children how to
  color and cut them out.
• Have an adult volunteer complete the students' Pointer Pals as
  described in the Introduction.

Pointer Pal Patterns ⫸

Rocks, All Kinds of Rocks

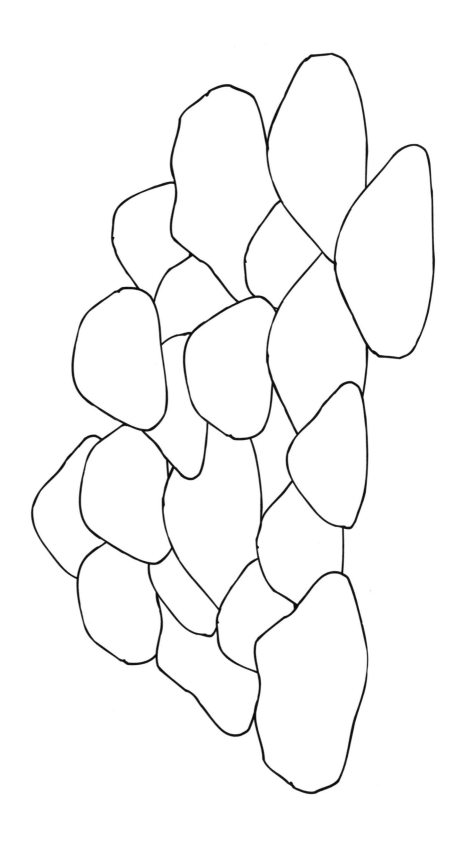

I like rocks, all kinds of rocks.

1.

I like big rocks.

2.

I like little rocks.

3.

I like shiny rocks.

4.

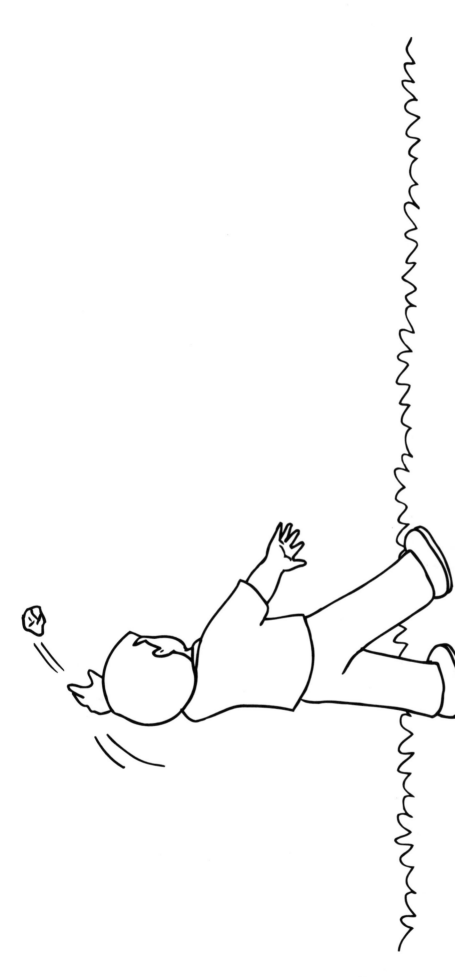

I like round rocks.

5.

I like to throw rocks.

6.

7.

Center Connections ©1998 Monday Morning Books, Inc.

Rocks, All Kinds of Rocks

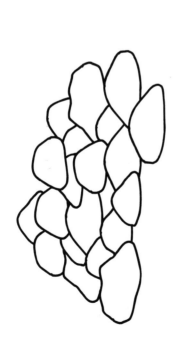

I like rocks, all kinds of rocks.

1.

I like big rocks.

2.

I like little rocks.

3.

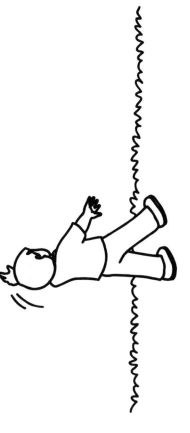

I like shiny rocks.

4.

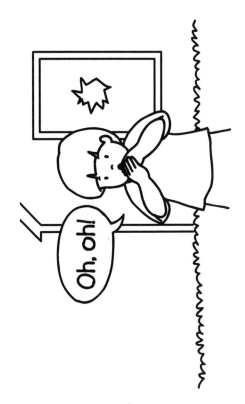

Oh, oh!

I like round rocks.

5.

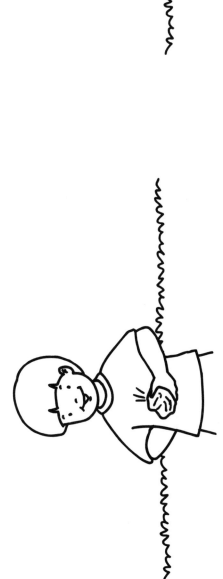

I like to throw rocks.

6.

7.

SEA LIFE

Circle Time

Ask the children to help you make a list of as many ocean creatures as they can think of. List the animals by size on a large piece of blue butcher paper, from the largest on top to the smallest on the bottom. Ask questions such as "Can you think of a sea animal that has eight legs?", "Do you know the name of a sea creature that has a shell?", "Do you know one that has sharp teeth?", "Can you name a sea animal that is shaped like a star?", and "Think of the sea animal that is named after a fruit spread that tastes good in a peanut butter sandwich." Post the list on the wall during the study of sea life and add to it as the children learn about more sea creatures.

Explain the center activities to the children.

Book List

Animals of Sea and Shore by Illa Podendorf (Children's Press, 1982).

A House for Hermit Crab by Eric Carle (Picture Book Studio, 1987).

The Ocean Alphabet Book by Jerry Pallotta (Charlesbridge, 1986).

The Seashore Book by Charlotte Zolotow (Harper Collins, 1992).

Swimmy by Leo Lionni (Pantheon, 1969).

A House for Hermit Crab

Materials

At least one copy of the book *A House for Hermit Crab* by Eric Carle
Listening post and earphones
Cassette recorder and blank cassette tape
Drawing paper and crayons

Teacher's Notes

- Tape the story and gather the materials.
- Prepare and display the center poster.
- Explain what the children are going to do when the story is finished.

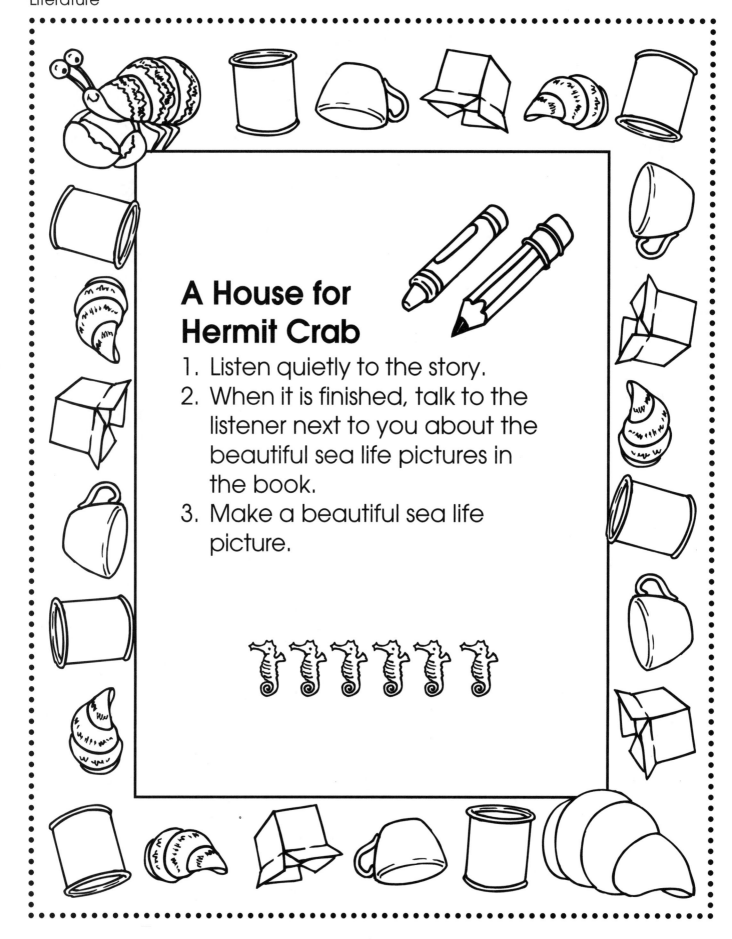

A House for Hermit Crab

1. Listen quietly to the story.
2. When it is finished, talk to the listener next to you about the beautiful sea life pictures in the book.
3. Make a beautiful sea life picture.

Tide Pools

Materials

Paper plates
Shell-shaped macaroni
Blue tempera or watercolor paint
Colored paper muffin cup liners
Colored construction paper
Scissors
White glue

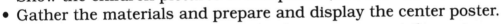

Teacher's Notes

• Explain that tide pools are tiny pools of water left in the rocks along the seashore when the tide goes out. Many little animals, such as sea anemones that look like flowers, sea stars, and many kinds of animals with shells, live crowded together in these pools. Show the children pictures of tide pools. (See the "Go Fish" cards.)

• Gather the materials and prepare and display the center poster.

• Show the children how the materials can represent the various creatures in a tide pool.

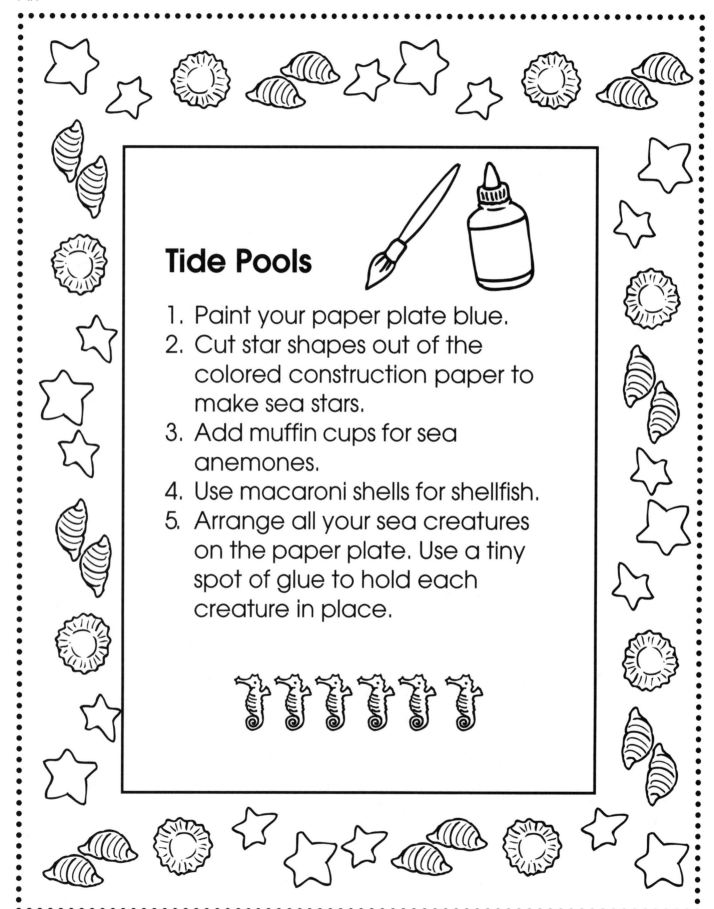

Tide Pools

1. Paint your paper plate blue.
2. Cut star shapes out of the colored construction paper to make sea stars.
3. Add muffin cups for sea anemones.
4. Use macaroni shells for shellfish.
5. Arrange all your sea creatures on the paper plate. Use a tiny spot of glue to hold each creature in place.

Fish Food

Materials

Fish-shaped crackers or patterns
"Fish Food" work mat
Small paper cups

Teacher's Notes

- Make five or six copies of the work mat. Color and laminate them.
- Review counting with the children, then demonstrate the activity.
- Show the children how to "feed the fish." Fit one layer of the fish-shaped crackers or patterns inside the designated area in each of the sea creatures on the work mat.
- Gather the materials and prepare and display the poster.

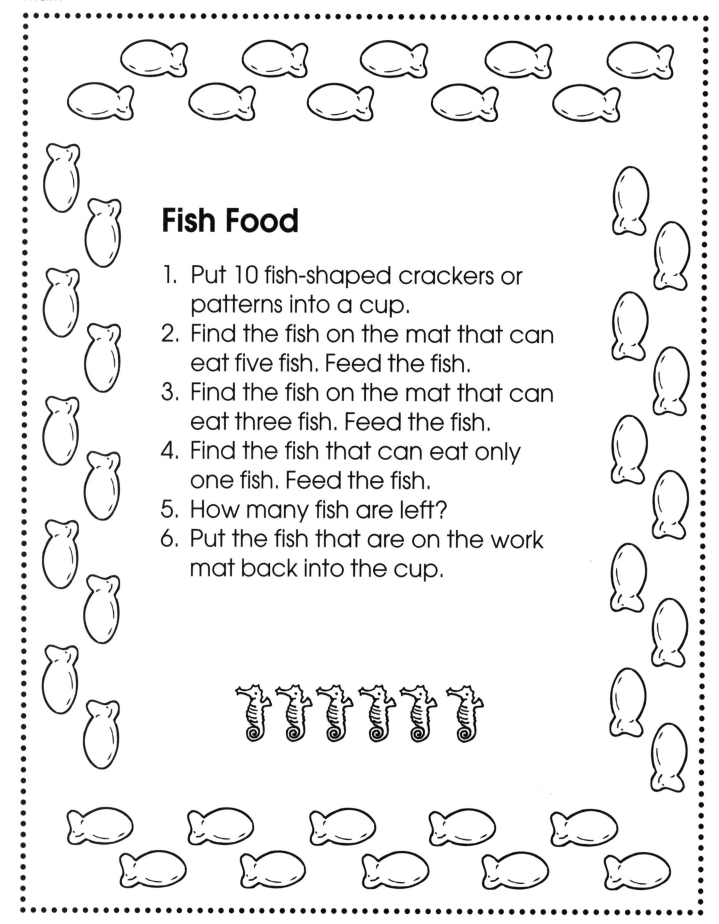

Fish Food

1. Put 10 fish-shaped crackers or patterns into a cup.
2. Find the fish on the mat that can eat five fish. Feed the fish.
3. Find the fish on the mat that can eat three fish. Feed the fish.
4. Find the fish that can eat only one fish. Feed the fish.
5. How many fish are left?
6. Put the fish that are on the work mat back into the cup.

Fish Food Mat

Fish Food

Name _____

Fish Food Patterns

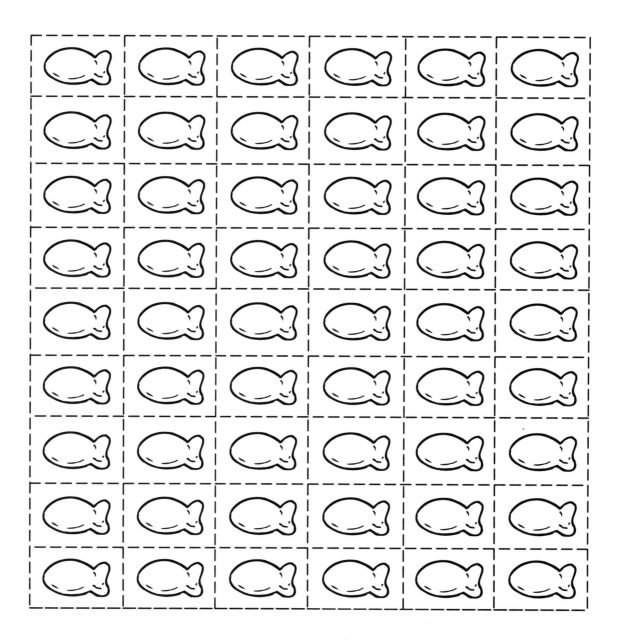

Go Fish

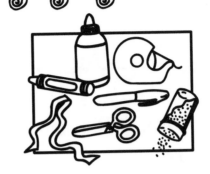

Materials

Activity pages of sea life picture cards
Lightweight cardboard or oak tag
Scissors

Teacher's Notes

- Make two lightweight cardboard copies of each sea life picture card page for each child.
- Prepare and display the student poster.
- Discuss the sea animals on the picture cards with the children. Be sure they are familiar with the animals' names before playing the game.
- Have the children cut their sea life pictures into cards. (Two of each picture yields one deck of cards.)
- Show the children how to play the card game "Go Fish" in pairs using one deck of cards.

ray

octopus

dolphin

seal

sea star

crab

whale

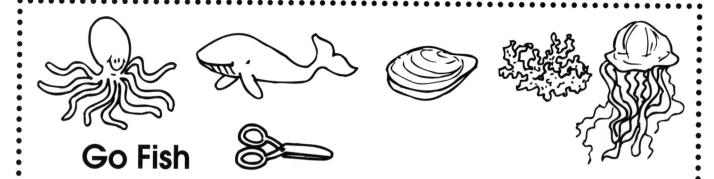

Go Fish

1. Cut the sea life pictures apart to make a set of cards.
2. Find a partner to play "Go Fish" with. Use one set of sea life cards.

To play:

- Shuffle the cards.
- Deal five cards to each player.
- Put the rest of the cards face down in a pile.

To take a turn:

- Look at your cards. Ask the other player if she/he has a card like one of the cards you have. Use the sea creature's name when you ask.
- If the player has the card, he or she must give it to you. If the player doesn't have the card, he or she will say, "Go fish!" Then you take a card from the top of the card pile.
- If you get a card that matches one you already have, put the two cards face up in front of you.
- Then it is the other player's turn.

Play until all the cards are laid down. The player with the most pairs of matching cards is the winner.

Go Fish Sea Life Cards

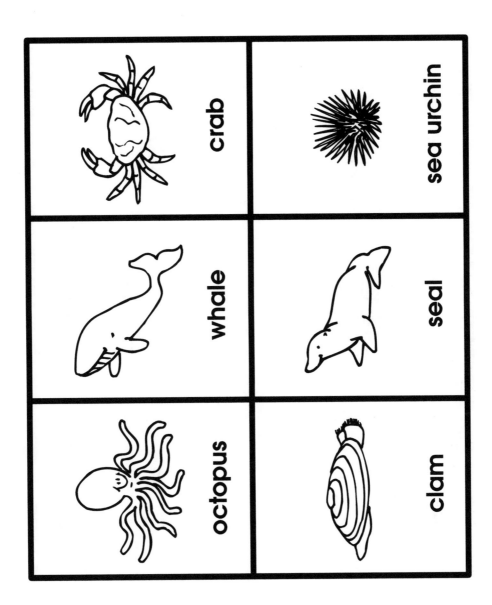

crab

sea urchin

whale

seal

octopus

clam

Center Connections ©1998 Monday Morning Books, Inc.

Go Fish Sea Life Cards

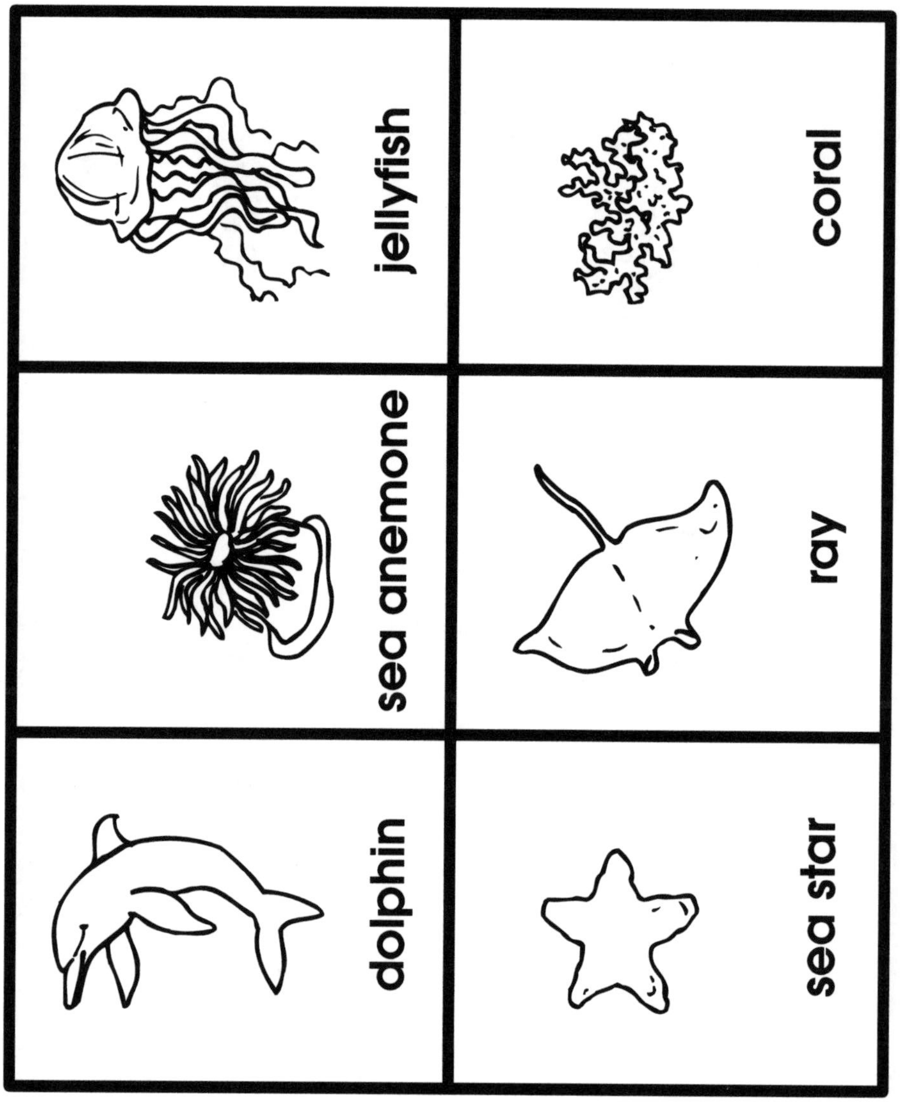

jellyfish

coral

sea anemone

ray

dolphin

sea star

Sea Life Counts

Materials

Student readers, 1 per child
Crayons
Aquarium sand
White glue
Tagboard copies of the little Pointer Pal
   pattern, 1 per student
Strips of tagboard
Cellophane tape
Narrow-tip colored felt pens for Pointer Pals
Lengths of narrow ribbon, 1 per student
Scissors

Teacher's Notes for Student Readers

- Make copies of the student readers and assemble one per child. See the directions for assembling in the Introduction.
- Show the children which two pages to color each day.

Special Touch: When the children have finished coloring their readers, give them some sand to glue along the shore.

Notes for Pointer Pals

- When the student readers are complete, put the materials for making the Pointer Pals into the Reading Center. Show the children how to color and cut them out.
- Have an adult volunteer complete the students' Pointer Pals as described in the Introduction.

Pointer Pal Patterns ⬤⬤⬤➡

Sea Life Counts

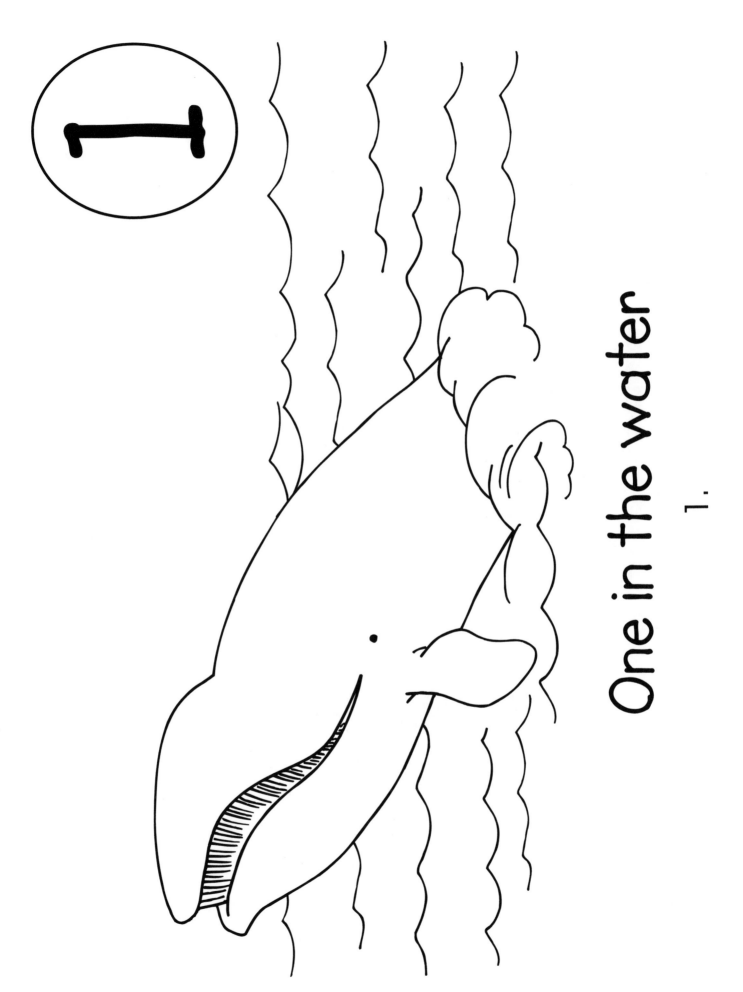

One in the water

1.

2

Two on the rock

2.

3

Three in the water

3.

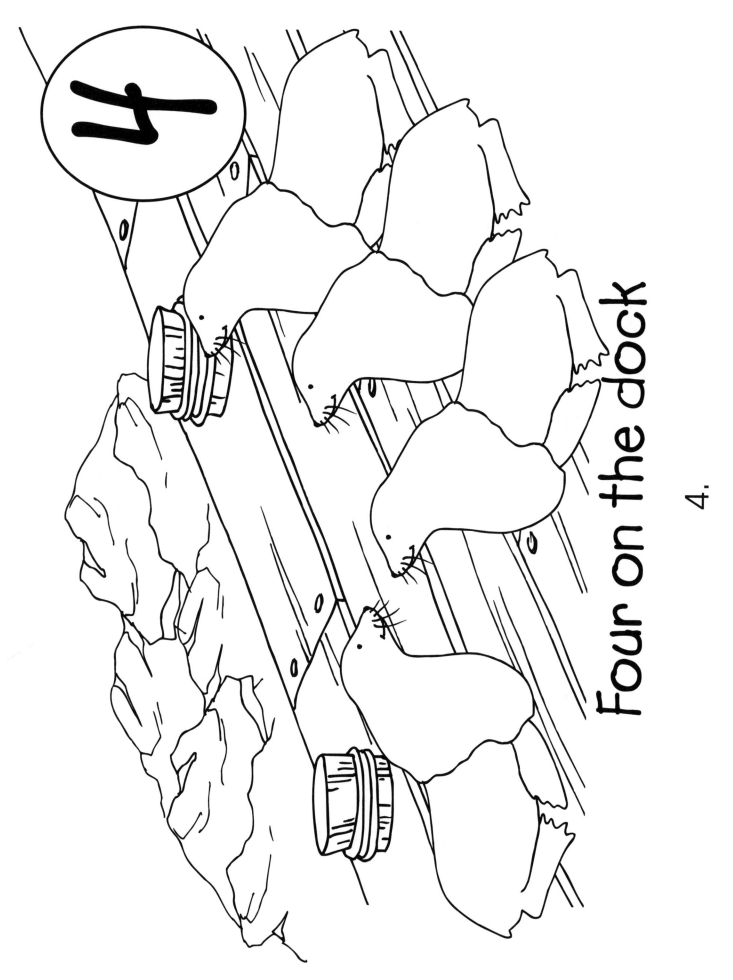

Four on the dock

4.

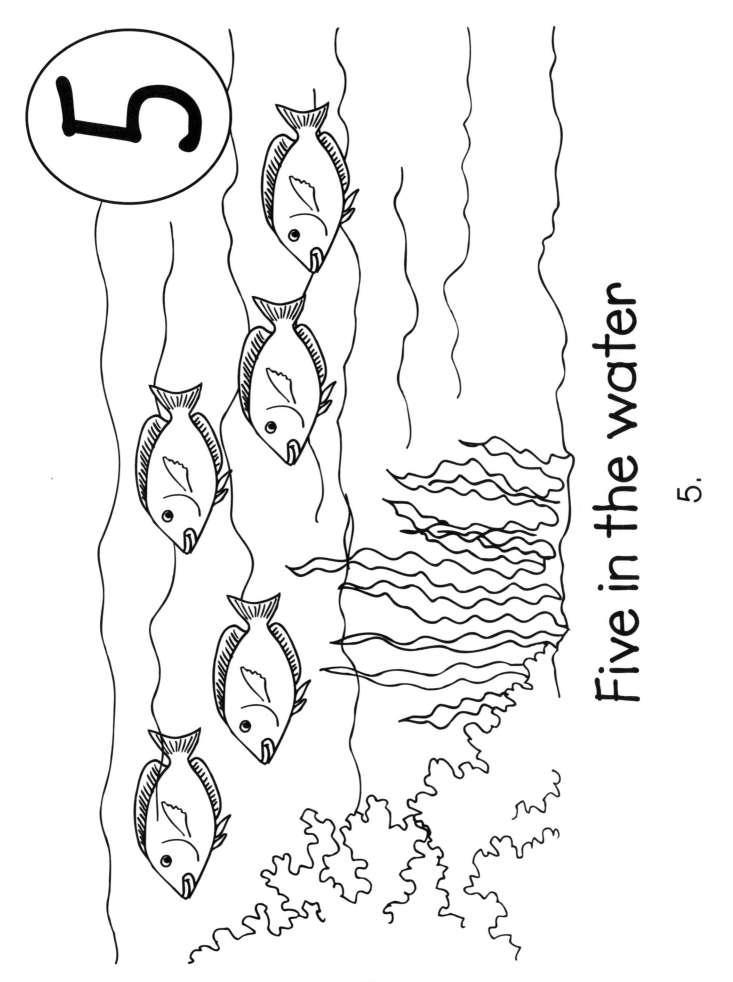

Five in the water

5.

Center Connections ©1998 Monday Morning Books, Inc.

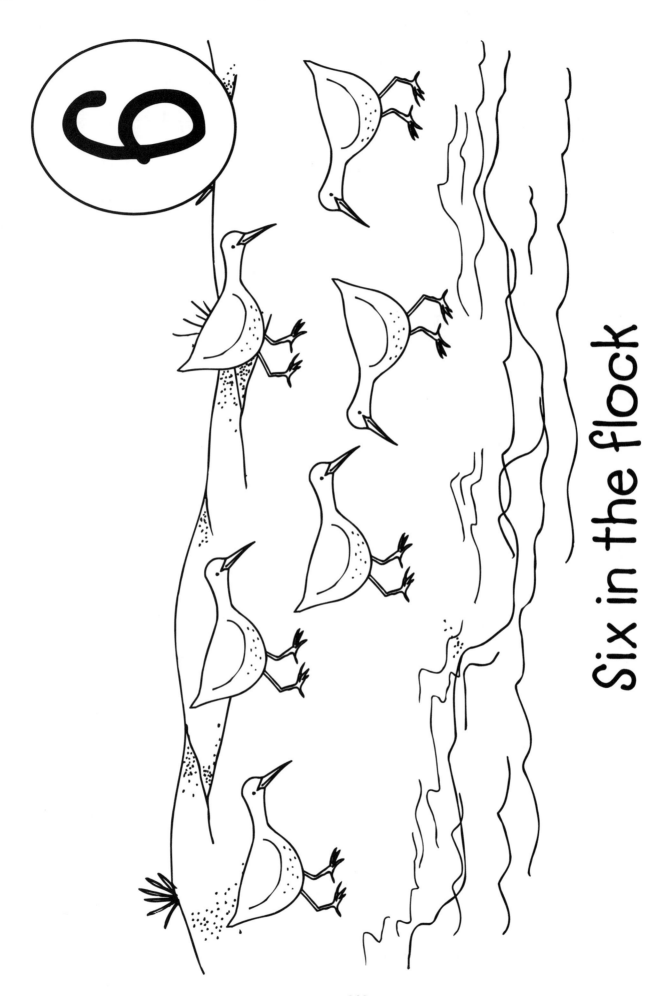

Six in the flock

6.

Glossary

4 Sea Lion	1 Whale
5 Fish	2 King Crab
6 Sand Piper	3 Sea Otter

7.

Sea Life
Counts

③

Three in the water

3.

②

Two on the rock

2.

①

One in the water

1.

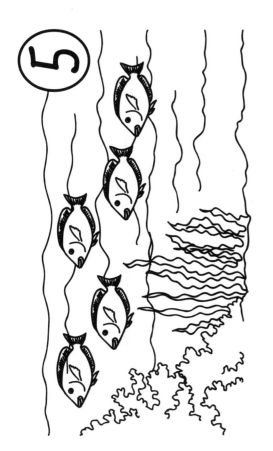

(5)

Five in the water

5.

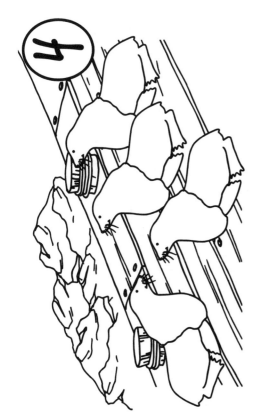

(4)

Four on the dock

4.

Glossary

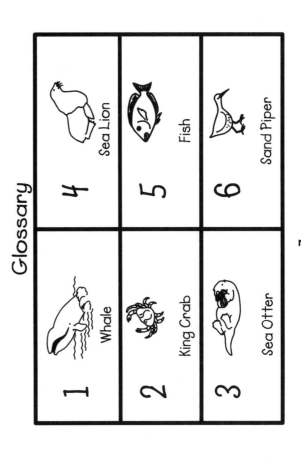

1	Whale	4	Sea Lion
2	King Crab	5	Fish
3	Sea Otter	6	Sand Piper

7.

(6)

Six in the flock

6.

Center Connections ©1998 Monday Morning Books, Inc.

About the Authors

Shirley Ross and Mary Ann Hawke
are kindergarten teachers
in Santa Clara, California.
They are the authors of
Alphabet Connections.